Best wishes

Brandon & Sharon.

Dorothy O'Neill

THE RULES OF ENGAGEMENT

THE RULES OF ENGAGEMENT

growing side by side

learning from nine couples
who made marriage work

Dorothy D. O'Neill, Psy.D.

Bookbaby Publishers
7905 N. Crescent Blvd
Pennsauken, NJ 08110
877-961-6878
info@bookbaby.com

Printed in the United States of America

This book is dedicated to my mother.
A woman who will be in my heart forever.
I wish you were here to share my joy.
Thank you mum, I miss you

ACKNOWLEDGMENTS

Well, where do I start!

I could not have written this book without the willingness of my couples to share their lives. For me this was an encouraging experience, and gave me hope in the success of marriage. Yes, it can work and these couples inspired me to tell their stories for everyone to read, thank you from the bottom of my heart, you know who you are.

I want to thank Dr. Alba Nino my dissertation chair for her dedication to keeping me focused, and the time she invested in me. My children, who lost so many evenings and weekends with their mother as I sat at the computer, while they bought me cups of tea!

My sisters and brothers who are so proud of me and tell me all the time. To Patsy who wants a shout out for making a suggestion. My dear friend Mari Jo who read everything and proofed and proofed, even on days she was too busy to help. She always made time for me. And to Devin, who came over to the house, reorganized the book, and questioned me to make it flow better. Although he had a full schedule at school, he was tireless in wanted the book to be the best.

And last but not least to Dr. Andrew Christensen who is not only a mentor, but has become a friend. Without his amazing theory that changes lives I would not have written this book.

Thank you all, I am blessed.

FORWARD

Unless you are a couple or family therapist, you don't get to look inside the marriages of others. You of course see your own marriage (or marriages) and may wonder if it is better or worse than those of your friends. You observed your parents relationship up close, but you were a child then and were not cognitively able to comprehend it well. Occasionally you may hear about the relationships of your friends or family members but typically you hear about those relationships when something important happens, either positive ("we are going to have a baby") or negative ("she is driving me crazy," "I think he is having an affair") and you get a particularly one-sided view at those times, especially during the negative times. You have probably read about marriages in novels or seen scenes of marriages and romance on TV or in the movies, but those are filled with drama to make them engaging and entertaining. You may not have a good sense of what the marriages of ordinary people are like. And you certainly may not know what simple, key principles might be a guide to their success.

In this book, Dr. Dorothy O'Neill writes about 9 diverse couples who have been married for many years and happily so. She interviewed them extensively and writes about their struggles, how they dealt with those struggles, and most importantly, what general principles can be deduced from these couples that might be applicable to you. The couples themselves are interesting and would make a worthy read on their own, but the general principles that O'Neill finds in the relationship of these couples provides some "take away" messages that can be helpful in your own relationship.

Dr. Dorothy O'Neill is highly qualified to write such a book. She is the most avid and enthusiastic student of couple relationships in general and couple therapy in particular that I have met. She conducted all the interviews herself of these couples. She developed an interest in Integrative Behavioral Couple Therapy (IBCT), an approach to couple therapy that Neil Jacobson and I developed (Jacobson & Christensen, 1998; Christensen & Jacobson, 2000). She has come to more workshops on Integrative Behavioral Couple Therapy than anyone else. She has done her own training of others in that approach herself. And I am pleased and proud that she used IBCT as a conceptual framework from which to view these couples. The result is not only a book that is interesting but one that is enlightening as well and one that may help you in your own relationship.

Andrew Christensen,
Ph.D

REFERENCES

Jacobson, N. S. & Christensen, A. (1998). *Acceptance and change in couple therapy: A therapist's guide to transforming relationships*. New York: Norton.

Christensen, A.. & Jacobson, N. S. (2000). *Reconcilable differences*. New York: Guilford. Note that there is a revised 2nd edition: Christensen, A., Doss, B. D., & Jacobson, N. S. (2014). *Reconcilable Differences*. New York: Guilford.

Contents

The Couples   *xix*

Introduction   *xxv*

Chapter 1

My Story   *1*

Chapter 2

Navigating the Difficult Territory of Finances in Marriage   *7*

Rule # 1: Organize finances early in the marriage, and have an understanding and an acceptance of each other's role in financial management   *8*

Jane at the Helm   *13*

Joint Accounts   *14*

Financial Security   *14*

The Time Share   *15*

Separate Accounts When Needed   *16*

Chapter 3

Managing Marriage and the Extended Family   *19*

Rule # 2: Have an acceptance through tolerance of the role of extended family and an understanding that the couple relationship comes first   *20*

Extended Family   *25*

Marriage First   *25*

Big Extended Family   *25*

A Close Family   *26*

Extended family rejection of your spouse   *27*

The Family Business   27

Thanksgiving   28

High Standards   30

In-Laws   31

Chapter 4

Co-Parenting as a Team   33

Rule # 3: Agree to make the rules for the kids that work for both of you, and agree for both of you to uphold the rules   34

Reflecting Learned Parenting Behavior   36

Parenting and Marital Satisfaction   38

Conceding for the Children   39

Parenting in Crisis   40

Boys vs Girls   41

The Blended Family   42

Parenting on the Road   43

Ruff Disagreements   44

Chapter 5

Family Dynamics   47

Rule # 4: The family comes first, and time together at home and outside activities are experienced as a family whenever possible   48

Making Time for the Family   50

Couple Time to Family Time   51

A United Family   52

Maximizing Limited Time   53

Highs and Lows   54

Chapter 6

Understanding There Are Differences in Who They Are   *55*

Rule # 5: Understanding and accepting, compromising and conceding, are positive parts of the relationship, and are not about losing, but about preserving the relationship   *56*

Making Decisions Together   *58*

A Learning Experience   *59*

Flexibility   *60*

Giving Each Other Space as Part of Compromising   *61*

15 Minutes   *62*

In Tune   *62*

Not Needing to Win   *63*

Avoiding Damage   *63*

Don't Sweat the Small Stuff   *64*

Burden of Anger   *64*

Giving Respect   *64*

Increasing the Love   *65*

Emotional Thread   *66*

Admiration   *67*

Public Affection   *67*

Health Scare   *68*

Chapter 7

Differences and Remembrance   *69*

Rule # 6: Remember the Past and How You Came Together as a Way to Accept Your Differences   *70*

Differences   *71*

Introverts and Extroverts   *73*

Plans or No Plans   74

Cultural Differences   75

Remembering the Past   76

Looking Back   76

Businesses   77

Staying in Love   78

Faith   79

Prayer and Decisions   79

Difference in Faith   80

Faith and Appreciation   81

Chapter 8

Acceptance through Tolerance as an Organic Process
in the Marriage   83

Not About Changing The Other Person, But Changing You   84

The Good Marriage, Making It Work!   87

Chapter 9

The Tools of Engagement   89

What Can You Do to Change Your Relationship?   90

Conflict   90

What Player Are You in the Conflict?   92

The Pursuer   92

The Withdrawer   93

Triangulating   94

What Kind Of Disposition Do You Have In The Relationship?   96

The Fuel On The Fire   97

Stress   97

The Emotions From Our History   97

Lower Your Guard and Be Aware Of Your Armor   99

What Can You Tolerate?   100

Learning How To Talk To Each Other, and When   100

When Do We Need Couples Therapy?   101

Forgiveness And Remembering Who You Fell In Love With
and Why   102

Clorinda and James Henry O'Neill   104

THE COUPLES

The reason I am writing this book is because I cannot believe, and will never believe, that every marriage that breaks up should have broken up! With an epidemic of divorce and broken families, we need to understand what works in couples that make it work; what are they doing that is working? This book is to help couples understand what they can do to stay married. I believe if more couples understand how other couples make it work, then we can stop the flood of broken homes and the hardship that comes with divorce. No one gets married with the presumption, "I will get divorced." Everyone wants their marriage to work, but sometimes it is hard to understand what goes wrong, or how to fix it.

I interviewed 9 couples to find out their strategies for success. The couples in this book have the same issues as the rest of us but seem to be able to get through the tough stuff and make it work! They were willing to share their marriage and family, life experiences. All the couples have been married over 15 years, have one or more children, have never received marriage counseling, and scored over 60 on the couple's satisfaction index (CSI).[1] The CSI is a questionnaire

---
[1] Funk, J. L., & Rogge, R. D. (2007). Testing the ruler with item response theory: Increasing precision of measurement for relationship satisfaction with the Couples Satisfaction Index.

that denotes marital satisfaction; a score over 60 puts the couple in a "satisfied with marriage" category. In this study, the average CSI score was 79. The couples were questioned about finances, extended family, parenting, everything from how they spent time together as a family to how they handled their differences. The couples' marriages ranged from 15 to 51 years. I interviewed the couples to find the answers to these questions: How do these couples keep their couple-relationship from self-destructing, how do they stop the escalation of the conflict, and how do they feel about each other after all these years? What can they teach us about making it work and staying together in a marriage?

25 Years of Marriage - Mary (53) and Adam (54) are a Caucasian couple of French and German heritage. This is their first marriage. They have 2 children, both boys (one in his second year of college and one a freshman in high school). Adam is an engineer and Mary, a stay-at-home mom. Mary has her masters in nursing but is not currently working in the field. They are middle class. Mary met her husband on a blind date that was set up by Adam's friend. It was New Year's Eve, 1984, however, they did not seriously date until January of 1988. They got engaged in March of 1989 and married in April of 1990. And, as Mary says, the rest is history! Married for life.

15 Years of Marriage - Carmen (40) and Henry (54) are a multiracial couple. Carmen is Hispanic and Henry, Caucasian. This is their first marriage. They have two boys (both in elementary school). Henry works in a machine shop, and Carmen is an office manager. They are lower, middle class. Carmen met her husband at work. He delivered materials to her workplace, and if she was not there, he would leave a candy at her desk or bring in her favorite drink and leave it for her. He would flirt with her and was attracted to her but was not sure if she would go out with him. After about 6 months, he finally asked her if she would go to lunch; They married 3 years later and intend to be married forever.

51 Years of Marriage - Betty (70) and David (70) are a middle class, Caucasian couple. This is their first marriage. David and Betty had 3 children: 2 girls (one married and another who passed away at the age of 7) and a boy age 50 (a controlled heroin addict). David is a retired CEO and Betty is a stay-at-home mom. They met in Kansas while both attending university in 1964. They both had friends in a student club and went on the same club field trip. It was a blind, double-date with David, Betty, and their roommates. David drove and had opted for Betty's roommate, but there was something about Betty's expressive eyes in the rearview mirror that caught his attention. After seeing those eyes, he was on fire! They did a roommate switch which has lasted over 50 years.

33 Years of Marriage - Sheila (49) and Jackson (50) are an African American couple. This is their first marriage and they have 2 girls (one in college and one working). Jackson is a plumber and Sheila is in accounting. They are middle class. They met in high school and dated for 6 years before they got married. Sheila knew he was the one that she wanted for the rest of her life. She recalls when she met him: she was young and didn't have a clue what her life was going to be but knew that he put her life in focus. It was his loving nature and kindness that drew her to him; she knew from the beginning that he would protect her heart and be a true friend. Oh--And he was also cute!

32 Years of Marriage - Maria (57) and Marcus (57) are both Hispanic; Marcus was born in Mexico to Mexican parents, and Maria was born in the US to Mexican parents. This is their first marriage. They have 4 children (1 boy in college, 2 boys and a girl working). Maria is the director of her own company and Marcus is a truck driver. They are upper, middle class. They met at work when they were employed at the same company. They rarely spoke, but after the company moved to a new building, their paths crossed more often. Maria thought he was cute but had not really noticed him until the move. Marcus had always noticed her and was attracted to her. For Maria, it was about chemistry; they were very young and did not think of anything but chemistry! He asked her out for coffee, and 8 months later they were married. As Maria says, the rest is history!

27 Years of Marriage - Shaan (56) and Azam (50) are both Pakistani and first generation immigrants. This is their first marriage and an arranged marriage for both of them. They have 4 children (2 girls and 2 boys, all in college). Shaan is a therapist and Azam an administrator. They are middle class. Since their marriage is an arranged marriage, it was a little different when it came to dating. Azam's brother and sister-in-law brought the idea of their union to his parents and arranged the introduction. Shaan had never seen her husband before nor did she know his parents. The first meeting was a dinner with both families. She sat across the table from Azam and they talked for a little while. They asked each other questions and she found him honest, charming and felt he asked insightful questions and took a genuine interest in her. Despite his delightful personality, Shaan did not feel a strong attraction; he seemed to her just another Pakistani guy, and this was just another typical Pakistani, arranged marriage. After they had a chance to meet, the parents took over with the questions about the families and the details of a match. 5 weeks later, after all the preliminary talks and questions were done, Shaan said yes. The major influence on Shaan's decision was her grandparents; they wanted the union and that was the seal of the marriage. After 2 months, they were engaged. 1 year and 3 months later, they were married. She had only seen him twice after the first dinner, and that was with her parents. Nevertheless, they spoke every day on the phone and started building the love that they have to this day for each other. 27 years later, they look forward to a long life together.

17 Years of Marriage - Jane (52) is a Caucasian woman, and Gabriel (53) is a first-generation, Mexican American man.

This was a second marriage for both of them. They have 4 children from their previous relationships, all of whom are working. The children were 8, 10, 13 and 14 years old when Jane and Gabriel married. Gabriel is an engineer and Jane is a professor. They are middle class. Friends thought they were a match made in heaven and introduced them at a church function. They had coffee together. It was love at first sight for Jane. For Gabriel, it took a little longer—about a week! A year later they were married.

25 Years of Marriage - Daisy (60) and Ben (52), (Canadian) are a Caucasian couple of Scottish and English descent. This is Daisy's first marriage and Ben's second. They have one adult son. Daisy is an interior designer and Ben is in sales. They are middle class. Daisy worked for a design firm in the US which sent her to Canada to work on projects in different furniture stores. Ben worked at one of these stores in a small town. While Daisy was working, Ben invited her to have a cup of tea. After she accepted, he asked her if he could take her to a dance at the local hockey rink, and she said yes! Daisy found him to be very kind, sweet, and quiet. Although they lived in different countries, it didn't stop their relationship from blossoming. They started a long-distance relationship during the time you had to pay for long distance calls, so it was very expensive when they would sit on the phone for hours! They would see each other every couple of months; Ben would travel to where she worked in his part of Canada, and Daisy would make sure to return to the store where he worked. They married after a year and a half of dating and Ben moved to the US.

26 Years of Marriage - Rosa (50) and Ruben (51) are a Hispanic couple. This is their first marriage. Rosa is a school health-clerk and Ruben is a manager. They are middle class. They have 3 children, 2 boys (both in college) and 1 girl (in elementary school). They met at Ruben's cousin's birthday party; a friend of Rosa's had invited her. Rosa thought Ruben was a nice guy and talked to him at the party, but it was his beautiful smile that kept her interested that evening. Although Ruben did call the next day, Rosa was not ready to date. It was a few months before they started going out. 4 years later, they were married and had a beautiful family, which was what they both wanted. 26 years later, Rosa still loves that smile!

INTRODUCTION

Happy marriages bring many benefits to a couple, and also to the family as a whole. Not only is there a sense of success in keeping a marriage together, but a physical and emotional well-being as well. There is evidence that marital satisfaction is one of the best predictors of overall life satisfaction.[2] Happily married couples report better mental and physical health. Hence understanding what keeps couples together in satisfying relationships plays an extremely important role in society. Not to mention the health and happiness of the children.

Today, there is an epidemic of marriages that don't make it. Current divorce legislation has made it easier now than ever for couples to end their marriage. While this allows for individuals to leave unhealthy, oppressive, and violent marriages, it has also created an environment where couples with savable marriages tend to give up on finding ways to resolve their conflicts and misunderstandings. Instead, they choose a swift end and find the fast path to concluding their relationships. This is understandable; it may be easier to opt for divorce rather than look at each other's differences and find a greater understanding. However, when couples

---

[2] Cui, M., & Fincham, F. D. (2010). The differential effects of parental divorce and marital conflict on young adult romantic relationships.

do not seek to learn acceptance through tolerance, they end up in a no-win situation. There is a misconception that when a couple is faced with conflict there are two choices: stay in an unhappy marriage or leave. However, there is an overlooked, third choice: understand that conflict is often a salient misunderstanding of differences and find an opportunity to resolve the conflict.

When a couple is able to see problems as understandable differences between two partners, rather than give into submissive resignation to the problem, there is a chance for resolution. When a couple can let go of trying to change the other person in the relationship, the problem becomes a window into each other's vulnerability. Understanding differences does not mean that a spouse is always accepting without question, however, there is the ability to understand without the need to continue the conflict.

The couples in this book all had similar experiences when it came to finances, time spent together, parenting, compromising, extended family, respect of their differences, and reflections on the past. I have included their stories to share with you ideas that you may want to use in your own marriage and to show you that you are not alone in your marital struggles. 6 areas were identified as strong definers of keeping the couple relationship whole and on the right track.

Six areas were identified in this research as being facilitators of increased marital satisfaction: (1) couples organized their finances early in the marriage and had an understanding of their role in financial management; (2) there was an acceptance of the extended family, and an understanding that the couple relationship came first; (3) there was respect and acceptance of each other's role as parents and an ability to work through the differences, even if difficult; (4) the family came first, and time together at home and outside activities were

experienced as a family; (5) they believed compromising or conceding was not about losing, but about preserving the relationship; (6) the couples respected each other's differences and appreciated each other's recollections of the past.

CHAPTER 1

My Story

I am a product of divorce. After only 7 years of marriage, my husband, Ron, filed for divorce. But I believe, if I understood the rules of engagement while married or before, I might still be married. What is ironic, though, is that Ron and I have remained friends and work well together as a divorced couple. We even live across the street from each other! The very issues that we used to fight about were removed when we got divorced, and the rest of the relationship just worked itself out. The very areas that created the conflict in our marriage have now been processed with an accepting tolerance and understanding. We have changed how we see each other, and it has made for a relationship as parents, as people that respect our extended families, and as friends.

Why do we give up and get divorced? I can say that for my marriage, there was a severe misunderstanding of who we were as individuals.

We meet someone and believe, "this is my life partner." We get married with full intentions of staying together. Life could not be better! And then we realize that we have differences, differences that we have never talked about or have even been aware of. Differences that might, in the beginning, have been cute or sweet, but become the very issues that divide us and push us apart.

I came from poverty. My father died when I was 7 years old, and I was one of 8 children. We were all very young when Dad died. My youngest sister was only 2 and my oldest only 14 years old. It was a very tough life. We lived in a house without an inside bathroom and just a cold tap for water. Those days were hard. On Fridays, we carried the tin tub in from the garden and Mom filled it up with hot water from the boiler, then we took our weekly bath. Although the house was clean we had very few material items. The floor-boards were bare and the windows let in all the drafts on a cold winter day.

I remember going to bed and pulling up the old, surplus, army blankets to keep me warm. We had no heating in the house other than the coal fire in the living room that only burned in the evening until we went to bed and a paraffin stove that was on to keep us warm in the morning. I remember, in the winter, scratching my name in the ice that formed on the inside of the window pane and writing messages to my dad who had passed away.

It was a hard life. Although we had a loving mother, there were no luxuries beyond the bare necessities. We did not have new clothes and Mom could not afford expensive holidays. We had clothes from the jumble sale and shoes that sometimes had to have cardboard put inside so they lasted a little longer. Mom bought second-hand sweaters, washed and unraveled them, steamed them in a colander to get the kinks out and knitted new sweaters from the old wool.

When it came to extended family, I really did not have an experience or understanding of what that meant. I grew up with an Italian mother in England. Mom met Dad during the liberation of Italy in 1945. A few weeks later, they married in Naples and honeymooned in Rome. After the honeymoon, Dad hid her on a troop train to bring her back into England.

Being an Italian in England after World War II was not an ideal situation. Even though my father had many sisters and brothers, they did not embrace a foreigner. In addition, all her family remained in Italy, so our exposure to extended family was limited. For us, there were a few trips to see the Aunts and Uncles in London and also a couple of times we went to the seaside with them. However, the bulk of our time was spent with our mother. Dad would experience his extended family by leaving us at home with Mom and traveling up to London on his own. On rare occasions, they would come to Epsom where we lived (20 miles from London) and visit. After Dad died we hardly saw them.

So, we were just a family that lived together—all 9 of us! We had two visits from Italy in all the time Mom was alive and living in England. We never knew what it was like to pop into an aunt or uncle's house or play with cousins. We had no idea what it meant to share Christmas and time with extended family. All our holidays and celebrations were as the immediate family. There were no decisions of whose family to go to, as we were the family.

Not only did I experience poverty and a lack of extended family, I experienced not knowing what a couple relationship should look like. Growing up without a father, there was only our tireless mother to take care of us. Our mother did not date or go out; she kept the home safe and her children safe. I learned from her what you did to care for your family and how to make decisions on your own. I had no idea how you shared in a relationship with a spouse or how compromising worked. She taught me to be a strong woman when it came to being self-sufficient and she taught me how to manage alone. Managing alone was the norm for me and I did it so well. I was able to do all the things my mother did and more. There was no missing piece or sense that this was not normal. It functioned like clockwork because it was what I knew and what I had learned.

I never knew my father so I had no idea what differences my parents had, what got them into a fight, or even what made them laugh. I had no example of working through differences or how to navigate out of and de-escalate conflict with a spouse. My world was one dimensional when it came to relationships. I only saw what hard work was, and how to do it by being a one-man show. When Dad died, the welfare department asked Mom to give up half her children as they believed it was too much for one person. This would have been an easy way to avoid the struggle and hardship of single parenthood. However, her understanding of being a mother was that you took care of your children from the day they were born. Parenting was an important part of who she was and performing her role as a parent was the most important part of her life. Needless to say, she did not give up her children. While I did not have an example of a couple relationship, I learned about taking care of the children and parenting.

We did not see intimacy and how intimacy was meant to be worked out between loving, married couples. We had no idea how a couple would interact in a warm and personal way with each other. We missed out on seeing the flirtatious play of a couple and the gentleness of caring for your spouse. A simple gesture such as holding hands, or the welcome home kiss, was never part of our experiences of what a relationship looked like. We never saw a cuddle on the couch or the care and attention of a spouse when the other was sick.

I had a skewed understanding of relationships from limited experiences of seeing my friends' parents and witnessing the easy, blissful lives of sitcom couples. I saw only the shadow of a couple relationship and I had the idea that all was bliss. I wondered about having a dad and about the seemingly simple life of a couple, full of love and adoration.

These simple experiences that are part of a couple relationship were all absent in my learning—or lack thereof—about marriage. It is not surprising that I had no idea what to do or how to understand my role when I was married. It is also not surprising that I had constant disappointment and rejection in my marriage. I was often deeply hurt and angry at the very things I did not understand and at the idea that this marriage was not what I believed marriage was meant to be.

I picked a man that, although he came from 2 parents, came from parents that were not outwardly affectionate towards each other, nor did they address each other's differences. They did the parenting role but did not display the emotions toward each other that project the image of a couple relationship. They were his example of a married couple and taught him their behaviors. I believe I picked Ron and he picked me because we had similar deficits and strengths. We both had not experienced intimacy and came to the marriage with different understanding and needs. We were a recipe for disaster!

As a marriage and family therapist, I have had years of schooling and training to understand what went wrong in my marriage. Although I cannot go back, I have the ability to help others see what is taking place in their marriage and in the decisions they make. I am now aware that we have many areas of our lives to look at, and we need to understand how these mesh with the one person we choose to spend our lives with.

We are a product of learned behavior and misunderstanding of what to expect in marriage. I decided when choosing a thesis for my doctorate to look at what worked in couples that stayed married and reported a happy marriage. It was through my research that I realized there were rules of engagement for a healthy marriage, and these rules were present in all the couples I interviewed. These rules were consistent and were the foundation of why they could all find happiness and security in their marriage. Simply put, these rules were the foundation of why the marriage worked!

These 6 rules will be the topic of the chapters. Again, I wish I had known these rules when I was married and I hope that understanding how the couples in my research made it work will help other couples stop the flow of divorce and the breakup of the family.

CHAPTER 2

Navigating the Difficult Territory of Finances in Marriage

Rule # 1:

**Organize finances early
in the marriage, and
have an understanding
and an acceptance of
each other's role in
financial management**

In this chapter you will meet:

- *Jane and Gabriel, Caucasian woman and first-generation, Mexican-American man 17 Years of Marriage*

- *Adam and Mary, Caucasian couple 25 Years of Marriage Ruben and Rosa, Hispanic couple 26 Years of Marriage*

- *David and Betty, Caucasian couple 51 Years of Marriage*

• *Daisy and Ben, Caucasian couple 25 Years of Marriage*

Financial decision-making is one of the most difficult areas of a relationship. The understanding that both members come with different financial agendas is not often talked through in the beginning of a relationship. There is this unspoken and wishful expectation that it will just work. Many battles are fought over money and spending in a marriage. Many couples start their path towards divorce over the difference and misunderstanding of how each of them sees spending and saving. Though this does not need to be the case, if not addressed early in the relationship labels start to be given to each spouse such as "spender!" or "tightwad!" Couples start the process of planning how to do battle, with the primary objective of winning when it comes to finances. How can they get what they want when they know their spouse will object? How do they work the system or learn how to take the fallout? How do they justify to the other why their decision is the best?

Understanding my financial role was one of the biggest problems in my marriage. We both came from two different styles of spending. In my family there was no money. A block of ice cream from the ice cream truck on Sunday was the treat of the week. I always had second-hand clothes and did not know what it was to have the luxuries that my peers had. Consequently, when I got married, I wanted to buy everything I desired, I wanted my children to have everything I did not have, and I wanted it all! On the other hand, Ron wanted to save every penny. He had been taught by a family that came from the dust bowl that if you don't put it away you won't have it when you need it. The message was, "Don't spend money unless you need to. Spending money on things you don't need is a waste!" So, you can see how we started the marriage with differences in finances and both believed we were right. We never had a conversation about what is the best way; it was only his way or mine!

The couples in my study had different ideas when it came to finances. Although they all came from different backgrounds, they all had the same strategies when it came to finances in the couple relationship. They all had similar systems within the marriage and they all made it work. The first thing most did when they got married was to combine their accounts. This was a very important part of establishing trust in the relationship and establishing that the money belonged to both of them, whether they stayed at home and looked after the children, or if one made less than the other. The agreement to have joint accounts was a way to establish what they had as a couple and as a family, rather than as individuals. However, while joint accounts are shown to be helpful, marital success in navigating finances can happen without them! Some couples have three accounts, one for each partner, and a third joint account for joint expenses. This allowed couples to work together, but also have some spending money without taking from the joint account.

The key was working together on managing joint expenses. Even without a joint account, some couples are able to have separate accounts and maintain a healthy relationship. The key is establishing trust, openness, and team work on managing the finances.

After establishing the accounts, they were able to allocate funds to different areas of their joint needs. They established one person to pay the bills but also acknowledged the need to check in with each other to what was being spent. In addition, any large item that needed to be purchased was always talked through, and unless a joint decision could be reached, it was not purchased.

I found that the establishment of who paid the bills not only de-escalated conflict, it strengthened the respect that couples had for each other. There was a trust and a safety that came out of this arrangement and an understanding of each of their responsibilities. Prior research has shown that allocating one member in the couple relationship to be the bill payer has worked in de-escalating conflict or misunderstanding.[3] Husbands and wives often view money differently and the way financial debt is handled is a known predictor of marital satisfaction. Establishing equal opportunities and fairness in the early stage of the marriage is a predictor of marriage survival. Research has shown that understanding the stressful, financial issues more compassionately, offering financial advice to each other, and equal sharing of the financial burden all have been effective in building marital satisfaction when there was a financial burden.[4] Equal sharing of managing finances may not always be possible, but a successful marriage is still possible if one partner takes on more of the management.

What these couples had in common was the lack of urgency to have just what they wanted. Buying something that was not mutually agreed upon came at a cost to the relationship. They had established an understanding that the financial good of the relationship was based on a mutual respect and being patient with each other when it came to spending money; the needs of the relationship came first.

In addition, these couples were very careful about what they spent money on. It did not matter what economic background they came from or how high their current income was, spending was thought through and based on what was best for the couple as a team. There were times when one wanted something the other did not and at these times they had to navigate through conflicting discussions. They did not override each other, but listened to each other make a case for their reason why, or why not money should be spent.

---

[3] Falconier, M. K. and Epstein, N. B. (2011), Couples experiencing financial strain: what weknow and what we can do
[4] Schaninger, C. M., & Buss, W. C. (1986). A longitudinal comparison of consumption and finance handling between happily married and divorced couples

During these times, one of them would compromise, however it was not a submissive compromise, but an understanding that this was for the good of the relationship. They understood pushing would only damage the relationship, and the relationship was worth more than whatever it was they wanted to purchase.

Money should be seen as how it can secure your future and strengthen the relationship

Studies have shown 4 ideas that establish an understanding about finances and a happy marriage. The first is the perception of joint decision making by couples. These couples are able to have a considerate discussion and agree to a mutual compromise to work through the issues rather than argue. The second is the ability to maintain economic security and adequate income. Economic insecurity places a costly burden on couples. The third is successful conflict management which entails having a higher agreement to disagreement ratio.[5] This means that couples should be able to accept the outcome of disagreements that do not reach a perfect resolution on. This does not mean that the spouse has to be submissive, but if they are better at compromising, then they should utilize their ability to compromise. Lastly, having a family commitment expressed by having an obligation towards the strong marital bond eases the tension of finances. A couple should always keep in mind that

---

[5] McGoldrick, M. (1999). Becoming a couple

their marriage and family come first and the way they handle their finances is a reflection of the care they take in their partnership.

Money should not be seen as mine or yours, but as a way to grow together and secure a sustainable future. Giving up on getting your own way when it comes to spending creates a team that wants the best for each other. This arrangement of couple finances strengthens the understanding that you want to build together, and that you care about the future. It is an understanding that creates a bond

Jane at the Helm

Jane and Gabriel managed their finances with Jane at the helm. Gabriel was able to admit that while financial planning was not his expertise, his wife had a thorough understanding of how to best manage their finances. All of their accounts were joint and they had an agreement that all large ticket items were only purchased if the purchase was not damaging to the marriage. Gabriel believed they recognized their strengths and weaknesses and was very aware he could do a budget and save as he had done this during his divorce. However, he felt no one did the bills better than Jane. He confessed he often did not know how much money they had but he felt comfortable that whatever Jane did she had a handle on it. His money went directly into the joint account and Jane went ahead and made the household expenses work. Gabriel had a hard time giving up control in most areas but he was able to in this area. In their family, Gabriel was understood to be the head of the household and consequently when he delegated this job he was still doing the job. They had both come from first marriages where there was not an understanding of roles but in this marriage they both felt they knew their role in the family and appreciated each other more because of this understanding.

Joint Accounts

Adam and Mary always shared finances. They started out young and from the same point financially, so their roles in the finances were decided early in the marriage. After 2 years of marriage and living in California they moved to Wisconsin. Living in Wisconsin gave them the opportunity to attend graduate school and still afford to live on their salaries. They left their home in California and ended up living in student couples housing which was a space of only 500 square feet! They had to be on the same page about money and organized about their finances so both of them could attend school. They believed they were a team, Mary the operations manager and Adam the bill payer. They always had a joint bank account and felt it was practical because if something happened to one of them the other would be ready to take over.

Financial Security

Ruben and Rosa allocated Rosa to pay the bills because of her accounting background and agreed that when they had financial decisions to make they supported each other. Rosa paid the bills online, and Ruben would check before the bills went out. Expenses were discussed so both of them knew where they were financially. In their relationship, when big items needed to be purchased, they understood that what they did in the moment affected the future of their financial security. Ruben and Rosa remember one instance when they wanted to redo the cabinets in their kitchen, but decided to hold off because they knew the stress from the financial cost would strain their marriage. When there were difficult financial decisions to make their motto was: "let's get it done together."

The Time Share

David and Betty had a shared bank account for their entire 51 years of marriage and they have both tried to be willing to concede to each other on big ticket items. In one instance, Betty wanted a time share, but David believed it was a waste of money. Betty believed they deserved a place they could go to every year as they had worked so hard to save for the future. David was against the idea from the beginning and said no. However, David saw how much effort Betty put into gathering the information on the timeshare and she had even signed them up for a free visit. David realized how strongly Betty felt and finally agreed to the time share. The relationship was more important than having his financial decision accepted. The time share not only worked for them, but they were able to take other people which increased their social time with friends. Even David enjoyed it! However, David believed credit card debt was the kiss of death and made sure Betty knew his point of view, and made sure they never left a balance on the credit card at the end of the month. They both compromised and were happy with the resolution of the disagreement.

**Spending and saving should be a joint decision
for the good of the couple relationship**

Separate Accounts When Needed

Daisy and Ben got married later in life, so they had already established finances differently. Unlike the couples that married young, they wanted to be more independent with their monies which for them worked. Though they had separate accounts, they were able to successfully navigate their finances and have a successful marriage. Because of this arrangement, they both paid their own, separate bills and shared the household account bills. They had an understanding that if one of them needed help they would jump in and pay what needed to be paid for the other person. Most importantly, they understood that they had to trust each other. Both had access to each other's bank accounts and at times when one paid for something the other would give money towards the expense without keeping track of the money given. Spending on all large ticket items was talked through, but it was not uncommon for Daisy to purchase items for the house without checking with Ben first. There was an understanding that she would make the right choices and spend only what needed to be spent. Ben believed and trusted Daisy even if he was not consulted.

During the recession Daisy's income was hit really hard. Normally she was able to pay her bills, but the lack of work in the construction industry took its toll on her ability to keep on top of her expenses, and slowly it became harder to manage. For Daisy, who had been so independent financially all her life, this was a place of anguish. However, Ben stepped in and helped Daisy manage her part of the finances. There was an understanding that they would stand by each other, and there was no criticizing or judgment from either if they needed help, there was a responsibility and concern for their financial security.

For all these couples there was the presence of a responsibility to their financial future. That did not mean they had to have large sums of money squirreled away, but it meant that they thought through spending and saving as a couple. They did not jump into large debt without the knowledge of what that would do to them and their relationship in the long term. Organizing their finances was seen as a way to enhance their relationship as a couple, not as a means of individual control. There was a healthy concern for the future and an understanding that future meant the two of them together.

CHAPTER 3

Managing Marriage and the Extended Family

Rule # 2:

Have an acceptance through tolerance of the role of extended family and an understanding that the couple relationship comes first

In this chapter you will meet:

- *Adam and Mary, Caucasian couple 25 Years of Marriage*

- *Sheila and Jackson African American couple 33 Years of Marriage Shaan and Azam, Pakistani couple 27 Years of Marriage*

- *Maria and Marcus Hispanic couple 32 Years of Marriage*

- *Ruben and Rosa, Hispanic couple 26 Years of Marriage*

- *Jane and Gabriel, Caucasian woman and first-generation, Mexican-American man 17 Years of Marriage*

- *David and Betty, Caucasian couple 51 Years of Marriage*

- *Daisy and Ben, Caucasian couple 25 Years of Marriage*

The role of extended family and the boundaries for the couple are often not thought through at the onset of the relationship. Even with healthy extended family, there is always a gray area of misunderstanding. What we think of as a supporting family member can be seen by our spouse as an interfering member, a caring parent as an over-protective or unaware parent. There are no relationships where the understanding of family involvement is completely established. However, for some there is an accepting tolerance and for others, a submissive tolerance. We often learn how to experience extended family by what we see growing up. In some families there is an open door policy, in others a need for an invite before coming over. For some couples, they would put their own plans on hold if the extended family needed something, and others would not think to change a plan that they had made for themselves.

I remember an evening during my dating period with Ron. He shared a house with his brother and his brother was nearly always home. However, on a rare weekend that his brother was going to be out of town, I planned a special dinner at his house. I took great pride in cooking and had planned this wonderful dinner with all the details. I had candles, music, the table laid out with meticulous care, and 2 fillet steaks ready to serve, when there was a knock on the door.

In walked Ron's cousin, right past me, while I was holding the cooked steaks. He went to the fridge, grabbed a beer and started to talk about car parts! The lights were down, the soft music was on, and I was standing speechless. He dropped himself down on the couch. Ron said, "have you eaten, we have steaks if not." I was shocked and overwhelmed that all my work had no value. However, what was really going on, which I did not know then, was that this was expected in his family. In his family, there was an expectation that one could come and go as they please and you always welcome them. No one needed an invite, you just dropped by.

Extended family is one of the most difficult areas to navigate as a couple

Extended family is a difficult area for many couples, for many reasons. We grow up within a family of origin that we often have total allegiance to, and depend on. We learn a system growing up that revolves around the order established by our parents. We interact with siblings in a way that is part of that system. We learn very early what is expected of us from our parents and what is for the good of this family system. Then we marry! We add a stranger that we have gotten to know and fallen in love with, and we decide to spend our lives with that person. Then we add that stranger's family to the mix. And we believe, quite innocently, it is just going to work…. Or we hope it will!

Extended family can be many things; they can be supportive, loving and demanding. How we navigate our new life with our spouse, navigate what role our own family plays, and what role our spouse's family plays, affects how our own couple relationship will work. It is not easy, but with the right rules we can work the extended family into the mix with a harmonious and accepting understanding all the way around.

In my relationship, the extended family was never talked about before marriage or during. My family all lived in England and Ron's family was local. When it came to family affairs or national holidays, he and his family assumed that it would be at his family's homes. There was no question or discussion about what that arrangement meant to each of us. I had no extended family here and although I loved being part of his family, there were no plans for us to establish our own patterns of interaction outside of the extended family on holidays or special occasions. There was only the need of his extended family and an expectation that you would be part of their plan.

On one occasion, I rebelled and wanted Christmas Eve at home rather than drive an hour to his grandmother's house. His family's tradition on Christmas Eve was at the grandparent's house. I wanted to establish a Christmas Eve that started a tradition for us as a couple. Although we did stay home that Christmas Eve, there was a fallout between us and also an issue with the extended family. On Christmas day there was a tremendous backlash from the extended family for not being at the Christmas Eve affair. This Christmas Eve tradition meant a lot to the family, and by not turning up, it went against the established expectation of the extended family. Had we talked about our needs, there would have been an understanding of our desires for the holidays and a compromise could have been reached to satisfy what was important to both of us.

A newlywed couple should have the ability to start their own traditions and establish what works for both of them, but the discussion of what that means, and how to handle the extended family, is paramount to having a successful relationship that works not only for the couple but for the extended family. When the extended family knows what your rules are, they can decide what they wish to do. The couple needs to have an agreement that they come first and the extended family will be worked into the relationship, rather than the other way around.

It is important to discuss what role the extended family plays as you both will have different ideas of what that looks like. How far can they go? And what is acceptable to both of you? When an extended family member oversteps their involvement in your lives how is that handled by the two of you? It is better to know the rules of what and how to deal with the situation prior to the situation arriving, rather than being caught off guard. An allegiance to each other must be first and foremost for a successful marriage. The role of extended family is a matter of discussion between the two of you.

Issues with extended family are not always about family traditions; they can also be about cultural differences. The number of interracial marriages today is growing which has created a blend of cultures (although that blend is not always harmonious). We have many marriages between individualistic and collectivistic cultures making the role of extended family all the more difficult. In an individualistic society, the couples tend to look after themselves and their immediate family. In a collectivistic society, the priority is the integration of the couple and the extended family. In the collectivistic society the interest of the group is more important than the couples own needs. In addition, interracial couples can experience peer and extended family pressure against their marriage, which in turn makes the contact with extended family tense and uncomfortable.

Extended Family

Marriage First

Jackson and Sheila resolved how to handle the extended family early in their marriage. They put no one in front of their marriage, and they did not allow the family to drive a wedge between them. Jackson made sure his family knew from the beginning that Sheila came first. This created a strong bond between them. They kept their problems inside the marriage and this helped them resolve their issues within the family. When extended family made demands on Jackson he told them he would listen to what they had to say, but they could not expect him to act on it if it harmed their marriage. On one occasion, when Sheila was in bed with the flu, Jackson's family wanted him to come over to spend time with out of town family that was visiting. He knew he had to take care of Sheila, and made sure his family knew his responsibilities. The extended family was livid that he would not be there; they did their best to convince Jackson to leave Sheila. They called and told him he was being stupid, selfish, and disrespectful for not putting the family first. They told him she was in bed and it didn't matter, that she wouldn't care or know if he was there or not. However, it did matter, it mattered to Jackson to take care of her. He knew Sheila would not be mad if he went, but it was not an issue for him, only for the extended family. Jackson could not be persuaded. He knew his wife came first and his responsibility was to take care of Sheila and his marriage.

Big Extended Family

Although Azam and Shaan had an arranged marriage and extended family played a large part in their lives, the extended family did not have an input into the dynamics of the marriage. They did not go against the extended family, but worked with the extended family to find a resolution when needed. Azam's extended family lived close, but he and Shaan both decided the amount of involvement. Both agreed that extended family was to be given the utmost respect and felt they received love and compassion from them. However, they established the ground rule that extended family would not be involved in decisions concerning their marriage. Azam did not like to drive the freeways and no matter where he worked, Shaan would make sure her schedule allowed her to drop him off and pick him up. One time Azam was only able to get a job in Bakersfield, (100 miles from their home). 3 times a week at 6 am and again at 9 pm, Shaan drove to Bakersfield to bring him home. Shaan's family felt this was ridiculous and told Shaan that he needed to learn to drive himself. However, every time they brought it up, Shaan respectfully acknowledged their concerns and was frustrated that this conversation kept coming up. She and Azam know what they wanted to do, and they did it. Shaan went about taking care of her husband's needs because she wanted to. To Shaan it was not a problem, although tired after work and attending school at night she drove to get her husband. When asked she would say we do things for each other and I want to do this for him. It is how we show our love and caring for each other.

A Close Family

Maria and Marcus had a different kind of extended family involvement. Although both from close families, Marcus's family was all gone except for one cousin who lived away, while Maria's was very large and lived locally. They established early in their relationship that Maria's family, which had many family gatherings and expectations, would be close and a part of their lives. This worked for Marcus as he deemed family a good thing. Moreover, they both agreed Maria's family would not interfere, no matter how close they lived. However, if something happened, Maria's family helped both of them. The extended family loved Marcus as a brother and son. They spent time with Maria's family, visiting each other's homes and if needed would seek advice, but the extended family would never give advice unless asked.

They felt they had healthy boundaries even though the extended family lived so close. They loved the extended family but decided early in the relationship that their own family came first, and they expressed this to the extended family. The extended family, in turn, was supportive and respectful. Marcus and Maria realized that Marcus being a part of Maria's large family was something they both wanted. Maria's family provided support when needed but were also able to respect boundaries. The relationship with the extended family was apparent when on one occasion Maria was rushed to the hospital unexpectedly. Maria's family rallied around Marcus and the children to give them all the support they needed. The responsibility of the extended family was to Marcus and Maria as a couple, not just to their sister. Marcus and Maria realized that being part of Maria's large family was a plus as they provided support when needed but were also able to respect boundaries.

Extended family rejection of your spouse

The Family Business

Ruben and Rosa experienced family rejection at the beginning of their marriage. They had to work hard to establish the separation of the couple relationship and the extended family. Ruben and Rosa came from different financial backgrounds. Ruben had established an affluent business partnership with his family and his family did not trust Rosa's intentions. There were constant tensions between Ruben and his family. Ruben came from a family of 8 brothers and sisters, unlike Rosa who only had her sister, cousin, and mom. All of her extended family lived in different states. When things got tough for Rosa with Rubin's extended family, she was advised by her family and friends to get a divorce, but she realized her husband had not done anything to her. He had always supported her, and it was an issue of how to navigate the extended family.

This is a perfect example of the power of the extended family on the couple relationship. Ruben always had Rosa's back and drew away from the family to protect his couple relationship. He believed the reason they made it was because he did not allow himself to pick sides, but put the immediate family first. It was not an easy first 2 years of marriage for Ruben and Rosa; the need to make sure the extended family did not damage the relationship was always present. Ruben pulled away from the family for these first 2 years and it was Rosa that brought them back together. Rosa wanted there to be harmony, and worked to build a bridge to the extended family. She would invite the extended family over, buy gifts for them, call them on the phone, have the children call their grandparents, and took the grandchildren over there. She never fought with Ruben about how the extended family treated them. She wanted the family to be whole and she knew this could not happen if she poured fuel on the fire. She was able to establish their relationship as a priority and still have a relationship with extended family. Rosa said that in the beginning her mother-in-law did not like her, but she never felt that she was alone. Ruben was always there to take her side. Ruben told his family, "Just because you are my family, I will not take your side against my wife."

Thanksgiving
Gabriel and Jane experienced pressure from extended family. Gabriel came from an involved, Hispanic family that lived close; Jane's family lived out of state. Gabriel's family believed marrying outside of the race was not acceptable

and his family made it very clear that Jane was tolerated, but not part of the family. However, no matter how hard Gabriel's family pushed Jane away, she made sure that Gabriel stayed connected to his family. The extended family was viewed as important, but they did not abide by the extended family's terms. On a particular Thanksgiving, Jane's mother fell ill, and they decided to go see her. When Gabriel's family found out, there was an uproar. Thanksgiving was always spent with his family. Gabriel took a stand and expressed that he had no control over how they felt about him going, but he was going for his wife. For Gabriel, the most important concern at that moment was the preservation of the couple relationship and the needs of his wife. On many occasions, they did conform to the needs of the extended family if it did not interfere with their relationship as a couple. This was an agreement they had established early in the relationship to keep Gabriel's family happy. There was an acceptance through tolerance and respect for the extended family. The extended family was not seen as the enemy, but as an extended family that had demands that needed to be evaluated by the two of them as a couple. Jane played a large part in keeping the family together. No matter how much negative pressure about their relationship they received from the extended family, Jane made sure Gabriel never was estranged from his family. She worked hard to call and include Gabriel's family and would go out of her way to say kind things. She chose not to look at the negative side, but to look for good things about the extended family. Jane was able to see the good in the closeness his family was striving for, rather than see it as controlling. In addition, she was able to see the holding on to a way of life that the extended family had was a part of their history and not a reflection of her. She was able to respect this rather than go out of her way to make it an issue for her husband. This gave both her and Gabriel the opportunity to leave any arguments about extended family issues out of their lives.

High Standards

David was one of 2 brothers who were very close to their mother. David's mother had high standards and believed Betty could never reach them, nor would she give Betty a chance to try. Betty said that David's mother did not think she was good enough, nor smart enough for her son. Betty did feel she was marrying above her "station" when she married David. His parents had money and education. Although there were times that Betty got along with David's family, she knew most of the time that they did not approve of her. David was his mother's favorite and when the Colonel (David's dad) was gone, which was often as he was in the Air Force, David stepped in as his mother's companion. Betty knew that David's mother would speak unkindly about her during these times, but David never shared these conversations with Betty. David's parents admired education, which Betty did not have. In addition to judging Betty, David's parents were also judgmental of Betty's family. Betty said she started to try and improve herself thinking this would meet their standards, but it never did. And after 50 years of marriage, she realized that it was not a good thing to have let them control what she thought about herself, or their marriage. David's brother also looked down on Betty and they did not get along. On many occasions the brother excluded her from functions and talked as if she was not part of the family. It was not unusual for him to ignore her altogether as if she was just an inconvenience. David agreed that Betty was in a much harder position than he was with regard to extended family. Betty's parents were different. They were laid back and did not make demands, and in their own way were intimidated by David's family. However, her family was always supportive and would do anything they could to help. They were humble while David's family continued to be judgmental. David had to work early in the marriage to set the boundary and put his wife before the extended family. By being aware of how important the couple relationship was and how fragile it was being made by family rejection, David and Betty made decisions to protect the couple relationship. And it worked, as 51 years later they are still married.

In-Laws

Daisy also felt she was not good enough for Ben's mother. It seemed she could do nothing right when it came to his mother, and felt she had to try and please her all the time. One Christmas when they were at Ben's mother's house Daisy was criticized by her mother-in-law every day of that trip. Daisy was criticized on how she wrapped the gifts, how she mashed the potatoes and even the PJs she wore. However, Ben's family did not live close, hence Daisy was able to remain polite with Ben's family because she did not see them that often. She was able to have an accepting tolerance during the short times she was exposed to the rejection from Ben's mother, and this helped their marriage survive. Ben was the baby of the family and although Daisy would get frustrated at the way Ben's mother treated her sometimes, she knew in her heart it was because Ben was still his mother's youngest and that she had a hard time sharing Ben at times.

Daisy's family did live close and they did not interfere; the extended family was easier for Ben. He was accepted into his wife's family as one of the group, and described the experience as being treated like a brother. Ben was included in all the outings the brother-in-law's put on. They golfed together, went on trips and to sporting events. Ben recognized that he had an easier time with Daisy's family than Daisy had with his family, and made sure to be supportive of Daisy when this came up. There was a healthy interaction with Daisy's family which included a separation of the couple relationship from the extended family.

Working with extended family requires a certain way of thinking about the couple relationship and the extended family. This is a very important part of the couple relationship and there is a need for the couple to respect each other, be united in how they view the extended family, and show the extended family that they are a team that works together.

CHAPTER 4

Co-Parenting as a Team

Rule # 3:

Agree to make the rules for the kids that work for both of you, and agree for both of you to uphold the rules

In this chapter you will meet:

- *Carmen and Henry Carmen is Hispanic and Henry is Caucasian 15 Years of Marriage*

- *David and Betty, Caucasian couple 51 Years of Marriage*

- *Maria and Marcus Hispanic couple 32 Years of Marriage*

- *Daisy and Ben, Caucasian couple 25 Years of Marriage*

- *Jane and Gabriel, Caucasian woman and first-generation, Mexican-American man, 17 Years of Marriage*

- *Ruben and Rosa, Hispanic couple 26 Years of Marriage*

Parenting is tough! As any parent will tell you, parenthood is full of stories that span from the baby days to the adolescent years, made up of both heartbreak and laughter. For many couples the transition into parenthood involves experiencing the unknown—no one gives us a playbook that works for our own family. Then we add work, worry, stress, and divided love between our children and spouse to the mix, and we are on overload, on a path to the destruction of our marriage. Parenting may be a full-time job, but trying to hold on to your relationship and keep it on track is also. This time in a couple's life is about being able to hang on to their own relationship while adding a new relationship.

Co-parenting is where the couples in the study had the greatest conflict. Every one of the couples expressed that this was where they had their greatest hurdles as a couple and had to learn to work through these challenges to protect the couple relationship. When a child can play one parent off against another then there is going to be a breach in the couple relationship. We know from studies that working together is one of the best way to have a successful relationship with the children.[6] Children respond better when there is a consistency in the rules and expectations. Although the situation might not be what we want, as parents, there has to be a unification for a child so they know where they stand.

---

[6] Pedro, M. F., Ribeiro, T., & Shelton, K. H. (2012). Marital satisfaction and partners' co-parenting practices: The mediating role of co-parenting behavior

Reflecting Learned Parenting Behavior

Couples enter a relationship with the learned history of how it was done in their own family. Some had very little structure and others a rigid or more controlled experience. We don't forget these learned experiences when we come into a marriage, or a relationship. Some parents don't want the same kind of experience they had when they were growing up to be part of their own children's upbringing, and others want it to be the same as their parents established. The parents that want it to be the same way often like the rules and organization of their childhood experience and believe this is the best and only way. The understanding for these parents is that "it worked for me and I turned out okay, so why not." Other parents will want to do the opposite of how they were parented. They often feel the control and expectations that they had to conform to were unrealistic when they were growing up, and they would not want their own children to go through the same thing. Whatever the case, this area seems to be the most difficult to navigate when children become part of the couple's life.

Co- parenting can create the most conflict between the couple

Both Ron and my experience of learned parenting was the same. There were household rules and a respect for our

parents that never wavered. The respect and boundary setting was established for both of us from birth, and we never questioned what this meant, or if it should exist. We had grown up with the pecking order in place and our parents instilled that in both of us. Hence, as divorced parents, we parented as a married couple would. Our children were very young when the divorce was final; they were only 2 and 3 years old. The first year was hard for me to keep a perspective on what was right for the children versus what I wanted in my anger at the divorce. I spent many days in conflict over wanting to make his life hard and yet wanting to protect my children from the perils of a bad divorce! It was not easy, as I am only human and was a woman that felt abandoned. However, the learned experiences I received from my single mother won out. Not only could I draw on the survival strengths I learned from my mother, I had my own motto: "love your children more than you hate your spouse and you will make good choices." This was how I balanced the end of my marriage and the start of a new way of parenting, one that allowed for the parenting to be healthy for the benefit of the children. Ron and I agreed to vacation with our children on occasion, attend their extracurricular events together, and remained unified in our approach to raising our children. We wanted the children to have the same boundaries we grew up with, and we instilled in them the ability to respect both of us no matter if we lived under one roof or not. Our children have never played us against each other because of the strong foundation we established early. They knew that we were united parents and cared about them deeply.

Parenting will never be easy, but three key strategies will keep the couple relationship healthy and allow for more effective co-parenting. Keeping importance on the couple relationship is imperative for the welfare of the marriage. That means not forgetting that, while you are both parents, the needs you had before having children still remain. Secondly, remember that we are a reflection of the way we were raised. You and your spouse should contemplate your own childhood and determine what you both want to keep and what you want to avoid in terms of raising your children. Lastly, to effectively co-parent, the couple must be on the same page. A united approach in childrearing will give the children stability and keep them from driving a wedge between parents. Whether that unity looks like establishing ground rules before having children or settling differences in parenting styles in private rather than in front of the children, it is important that the unity exists to keep the couple from drifting apart.

Parenting and Marital Satisfaction

Research suggests a link between co-parenting effectively when marital satisfaction is present[7]. Research also suggests that the transition of integrating a child into the marital relationship often creates stress that can lead to a decline in marital satisfaction. The dual role of parent and spouse often places additional stressors on the couple; couples have to successfully navigate how they will maintain both roles to achieve marital satisfaction rather than marital decline.[8]

The couples in my study reported that parenting together was an important aspect of their lives. They integrated parenting into their marital relationship by sharing time together as a family. Time was spent on co-parenting the children by attending sporting events, vacationing, and eating together. In addition, all nine couples reported that they had established rules and expectations for the children that were mutually agreed upon. Though parenting was the source of greatest conflict and struggle to compromise, they all agreed that they attempted to support their spouse when it came to child rearing by being accepting and tolerant of

---

[7] Froyen, L. C., Skibbe, L. E., Bowles, R. P., Blow, A. J., & Gerde, H. K. (2013). Marital satisfaction, family emotional expressiveness, home learning environments, and children's emergent literacy

[8] Rusbult, C. E., & Buunk, B. P. (1993). Commitment processes in close relationships: An interdependence analysis.

their differences. During these disagreements, there was an increase in discussions and an eventual concession by one of the partners; there was an understanding, even under pressure, that there needed to be a resolution. Although they were not always able to come to an agreement, they were able to concede without losing respect for each other. There was an accepting tolerance that this was for the good of the couple relationship, and ultimately the family. The couples believed that even in these difficult times, they were able to co-parent and stay connected as a couple. Parenting enhanced the ability of the couple to respect the competence and authority of their partner. Decreased attempts by parents to draw the children into a triangular relationship increased marital satisfaction. When couples remained connected through a mutual love for the children and each other, the martial relationship was able to successfully sustain the change in the shifting roles.[9]

Conceding for the Children

Most of Henry and Carmen's disagreements were in parenting. They had a big age difference and Henry's parenting style was more rigid. Henry grew up with a two parent family and had a strong bond with his parents and a very structured upbringing. Carmen, on the other hand, grew up with a cruel mother that neglected her and her younger siblings and often left them alone for days to fend for themselves. In the beginning of parenting, Carmen found it difficult when Henry disciplined the children. Because of her own childhood experience, Carmen's first instinct was to protect the children rather than discipline. However, Henry always appropriately disciplined from a kind stance. Carmen and Henry talked about their experiences and were able to come together as a team. Carmen deferred to Henry's style because she wanted her children to have a structured life,

---

[9] Parade, S. H., Leerkes, E. M., & Helms, H. M. (2013). Remembered parental rejection and postpartum declines in marital satisfaction: Moderated dyadic links.

even though it was difficult at first because of her own experiences. She respected that he was doing what was best for the children. Although they still had momentary impasses, they would talk through the differences in what they believed, and invariably, one would accept the other's decision.

Parenting in Crisis

At the start of parenting, David believed that fathers did not do a lot of the work. However, he and his wife had to be united when their son became a heroin addict during his teenage years and David quickly took a more active role. They described this as one of the most difficult times in their marriage. They had gone through the death of their second child and felt this may have been the reason their son turned to drugs. It was an emotional and draining time when they lost their daughter, and this was amplified when they had to help their son through drug addiction. They did not always agree on how to handle their son, and this caused tension in their relationship. David's family disowned their son, he was not allowed to go to their home and they removed him from the will. This was heart wrenching for Betty as she hated leaving her son out of holiday celebrations and visits to her in-laws. David thought the best approach was to lock everything up, as their son would steal from them for drug money. It was not uncommon for their son to break into their place of work or the house to steal. Betty felt David's approach was too harsh and tried to take a more nurturing approach. The discussions that they had were difficult and often ended up with them going their separate ways until they could process what to do. They realized that trying to solve this problem on their own was not helpful to their son and damaging to their marriage. They conceded that neither of them had the solution and sought out professional help to know what to do. Over the years, they paid for different rehabs, gave him money to live, paid for his accommodations, allowed him to live in the garage, and at one time, in one of their rental houses. All of these attempts failed to get him off drugs. As their son's problem continued over the years, the couple realized they had to be unified in their approach, and Betty decided to concede to David's parenting style for the good of the family and their relationship.

Boys vs Girls

One of Marcus and Maria's common disagreements was over the time their 17-year-old daughter needed to be home. Although they had similar parenting styles, Marcus was much stricter with their daughter than he was with the boys. On one occasion, their daughter was ready to go out, but Marcus felt it was too late. Marcus felt that she would not be safe going out at night and told her "definitely no." However, eventually, she was allowed to go because Marcus and Maria worked through the details of what their daughter was doing. Maria knew that to tell him he was just being overly protective would have shamed him and done nothing for the situation. She took the time to talk to Marcus, answered all his questions with respect, and helped him move in the direction of understanding that the girls were getting older and needed to do more on their own. Marcus did not lose his role of the parent because it was more important for Maria that they both understood how each felt and that they again agreed on the rules. Marcus realized that he was a reflection of the parenting he had seen in Mexico, where daughters had more rigid rules. While they did not always agree, Marcus and Maria appreciated that their perspectives were different, but ultimately the decisions that affected the children were unanimous.

The Blended Family

Gabriel and Jane had to navigate having children from previous relationships. When they first got married, Jane felt she bought more of a drill sergeant style into the relationship when it came to the kids. However although Gabriel felt he had been strict with his children and kept up with discipline, she felt he had a more warm and fuzzy style. It became a team effort, and she found herself being able to move more towards his type of discipline. They had a few ground rules to help the parenting run smoothly. When disagreements over the children took place, they would meet in private and decide on the outcome before talking to the children. They decided that Gabriel would announce their decision to the family, but all decisions on boundaries were made unanimously. Having a blended family, it was especially important that they made decisions together to show the children that they were one unit. Gabriel and Jane often had disagreements over how late the kids could stay up, who they could go out with, clothing, music, and sports. On top of this, they had to be wary of their children playing them against each other. Gabriel and Jane had to let their children know that when they grew up and left home, their marriage would still be there. At the same time, they let the children know that they loved them all equally. For them to make it work, they had to set their minds on making the commitment to stay married. Part of parenting was at the end of the day when all the stuff was taken care of, all the kids had answers to their questions, Gabriel and Jane would take time for each other. This was a time that the kids had to respect and knew this was also a part of the parenting rules. Gabriel and Jane had established a system they were both comfortable with. Because of the ground rules they created and the trust they had in each other, they were able to overcome the challenges of parenting a blended family.

Parenting on the Road

Daisy and Ben both traveled often for their jobs, and were in a different position than most other parents when it came to their son. They had many disagreements on how to raise their only child, and many times, Ben had to be the disciplinarian and make the rules alone. Ben and Daisy both had fathers that ruled with an "iron fist," and they did not want to raise their son that way. Ben's style was to take privileges away; he did not lecture or yell much. Daisy understood that, although it would not be her way, she had to be accepting because of the fact she was gone so much with her job. This was very difficult for Daisy, and many times she felt the discipline overly harsh, but had to step back and realize that because she was gone so much she didn't want any discipline when she was home. She just wanted to be able to enjoy her son when she was home and not have any upset. It was difficult to always be on the same page, but Ben and Daisy had to trust each other. They talked about their disagreements, what made each other feel validated as parents, and they reminded each other that they both had their family's best interests at heart. Daisy knew in her heart that she trusted Ben and believed it was not about the right or wrong way, but what was necessary given their circumstances.

However, on one occasion when Ben and Daisy were at the mall they had a disagreement over their son. Ben was watching their son while Daisy was busy looking at dresses, and their son got out of the stroller and started to run through the clothing. Ben told him several times to stop, but he wouldn't and finally Ben gave him a paddle on the butt. A woman standing near reprimanded Ben for hitting his child, and Ben retaliated by telling the woman to mind her own business! Rather than Daisy supporting her husband, she apologized to the woman for his action. Ben was frustrated, felt invalidated and felt that he and Daisy were not on the same page. Later they were able to talk about it and Daisy was able to see how it had made him feel unimportant as a parent. She again reflected on the fact that he had taken on more of the parenting role when she was gone. She also was able to share with him that she felt anxious that this woman would think badly of them as parents, and might call the authorities.

Ruff Disagreements

Ruben and Rosa often had disagreements over their children. One of these disagreements was over getting a dog for the kids. Ruben was adamant that they would not get one. He questioned who would take care of it, feed it, take it for walks? Rosa thought about the happiness it would bring the kids. They talked about it in private and finally understood why each of them felt the way they did. They were able to talk about the children's needs, and in the end, Ruben conceded that Rosa's decision was what was best for the kids. They got the dog! Ruben and Rosa had ground rules in place from the beginning, which helped them navigate the tougher decisions.

Making decisions together started early in their relationship. They felt that if they married and did not have a discussion of whether to have children or not and how to raise them, then after the honeymoon period, problems would surely begin. They both felt that being parents was very important to their couple relationship. They agreed to trust each other and parent together, even though they had different parenting styles. Despite their different parenting styles, they had the same core values for their children, and education was highly important to both of them. Even with agreement upon rules, parenting was still not easy—as parenting is never easy for most couples. They had a hard time accepting the children's transition into young adulthood, setting rules for different genders, and showing the children that their decisions were unified. These are areas of conflict that many parents have. On many instances, their sons would ask Ruben if they could go out when Rosa had already said no. They both had to check that they were on the same page because they believed disunity could make or break their relationship.

Their lives had revolved around the children when they were small, and they made sure they stayed involved as the children got older. At the same time, they remembered to take time for themselves as a couple in preparation for when they would be less involved in their children's adult lives. Ruben and Rosa loved their children and were both happy to sacrifice to give them the best life possible, knowing that eventually, it would be their time.

CHAPTER 5

Family Dynamics

Rule # 4:

The family comes first, and time together at home and outside activities are experienced as a family whenever possible

In this chapter you will meet:

- *Adam and Mary, Caucasian couple 25 Years of Marriage*

- *Sheila and Jackson African American couple 33 Years of Marriage*

- *Daisy and Ben, Caucasian couple 25 Years of Marriage*

- *Ruben and Rosa, Hispanic couple 26 Years of Marriage*

It is very easy to get caught up in the expectations of work, household responsibilities and the circus act of juggling everything we have to do. Many of us have the best intentions to do more than we have time for and believe we are doing our best. The demands on a two-parent family today are immense, and no one can deny that these demands take their toll on the family and the couple relationship. It is not uncommon for both parents to work outside the home, all the while having to navigate the family needs. Though not easy, finding the balance that fits your life is essential to the marriage and family.

In my marriage and divorce, the family was always very important. If there is one thing our parents taught Ron and me, it was family first. Being Italian, Mom was a great cook and meals were a big deal in our house. For her, feeding your kids was the way to show love. As I grew older I realized the significance of why meals were so important to me. The love was not about the food, but the effort and care put into this precious time to be together as a family. My siblings and I sat together for meals, watched TV together, and all played on the street together. Life revolved around our mom and time with each other. Little activities were special, not because of money, holidays, or rare occasions, but because we were present as a family.

In my relationship with Ron we never put each other or the relationship first. It was as if we were roommates at times and at other times strangers. I don't really remember many times when we made a joint decision. I had no idea we were buying our first house. Ron went to look at one and told me to stop by and see it. There was no discussion about whether we should buy a house and where. We were on a slippery slope towards divorce and we both had no idea. We went through the anger and the fighting that couples go through when one spouse files for divorce.... AND IT was not pretty!

However, after the rough part of the divorce was behind us, Ron and I were able to unite to provide a family atmosphere and family time for our girls. We could unite on parenting. Christmas and Easter were spent together at his parents' house with his extended family unless the girls and I went to England. Christmas was a time when Ron and I pooled our monies to buy the presents. I would go shopping and get all of the gifts for the kids and the family and then we would split the bill. Every year we went to the mall with our two girls and they would pick a parent to shop with and go off to buy the other parent a gift. It was one of our traditions and a lot of fun, and it lasted for many years. We had lovely Christmases. On Christmas morning, Ron would come over before the girls woke up and we put everything under my tree. The kids would open their presents every year with both their parents present. These times allowed our girls to see parenting as it should be, whether divorced or married.

All school activities were attended by the two of us together. Many people at the school had no idea we were divorced, as we were a happy family. Our friends remained both our friends after the divorce so we were able to attend weddings, funerals, graduations and parties as a family. We also ate together when we could, at his house or mine, and we would sit together around the table and share stories. It was a warm and good time. On two different occasions, we took the girls on vacation together. We were able in divorce to put family first, and it worked.

Making Time for the Family

In this study, some of the couples both worked outside the home and some did not. However, all of the couples were able to navigate a plan that gave them the most time together as a family. This time together came in different forms. For some it was sitting down as often as possible for dinner. They were all aware that, as the kids grew older, family dinners became harder and harder. In addition, in the younger years, the commitment of eating together and sharing their day was important in order to connect as a family, and that commitment laid the foundation for family time later in life. The extra school activities and sports were attended together as a family when possible. On the occasions that only one parent could go, there was time spent together after the event, at home, sharing the experience. More often than not, the couples worked their schedules so they could be there.

Most people want to put family first and realize the importance of prioritizing. With the complexities, overscheduling, and copious expectations of life today, there is no one-size-fits-all plan for family time and prioritizing the family. Successful ways that the couples in the study managed family time were family meals (especially in the younger years), taking vacations, visiting extended family, doing activities as a family rather than separately, and keeping work secondary to family if possible.

Try and fit in as much time together as a family even if you have to give something else up, it can always be done when you try

Couple Time to Family Time

Mary and Adam both prioritized family, so spending time together was very important. Time together as a family had always been at the top of their list of things to do. Because of financial planning early on, Mary was able to be a stay-at-home mom, which they both wanted for their children. Their time together as a family was going for walks at the end of the day which gave them time away from everything else. They had done this as a couple before children and incorporated the kids into this activity believing it was good for the family and important for the couple relationship.

These walks became even more meaningful because they involved their children. There were no phones allowed on these walks and they put the distractions of their lives on hold to try and enjoy time together. Mary and Adam were both present at the children's sporting activities. Adam volunteered as a referee for the boys' soccer so he could remain involved in their sport. There was a shared understanding that this made their family stronger. Holidays were spent as a family and consisted of simple camping trips and visiting family in other states. For their family, the most important thing was being together.

A United Family

Jackson and Sheila both felt that family time was an important part of their relationship. Sheila came from divorced parents, so her top priority was for her children to see a loving, committed family. Jackson was raised by a single mother and he wanted the children to see that a mother and father stuck together, no matter what. They found common ground in their childhood experiences and envisioned a single goal for their children: to have two parents that loved each other. They believed in eating together, spending time together, and focusing on the positive instead of the negative. They created a loving environment for the family. Jackson and Sheila spent time together every day by finding out about each other's day. This was a time to reconnect and it became a ritual that worked for both of them to decompress and share.

They made a plan after all the work of taking care of the kids was done, they would go to their room and sit together, making this time about them. They had developed this pattern because they realized they were not involved in each other's daily life; they were like two ships passing in the night. They made it work, and made time to spend time with each other and learn about each other, despite their busy lives. They made sure to keep their couple relationship strong so that they could keep the family strong and together.

Maximizing Limited Time

Daisy and Ben both traveled so much for work, and often at the same time, so their family life was not so straightforward. Family life was not easy; however, this was not a reason for them to give up on making the most of family time! They ate together whenever they could and always spent holidays together. Family time was given special priority when the whole family was home. The time they could squeeze in between work trips was appreciated and valued. They focused on being happy with the time they had together, instead of being frustrated about the time apart. After many years of not being able to have a vacation together, they planned a Disney cruise. This was a big deal as the family finally was going to have the vacation they had never had.

As they waited in line at the Disney ship counter to board the ship, Ben realized that his passport had expired! They all stood at the counter in shock and knew there was no way he could get on that ship. Ben tried to convince the family to take the cruise without him, but Daisy would not leave Ben behind. They decided to spend the vacation at the Disney Resort instead. They realized that they cared more about spending time together than a cruise. For Daisy and

Ben, family time was not about what they did, but about appreciating being together.

Highs and Lows

Ruben and Rosa had a strong understanding of commitment to family. They found joy and happiness in being married and having children. They ate meals together and attended the children's sports and activities. They also spent time in prayer together. At every meal, each family member shared their high points and the low points of the day. Ruben and Rosa had a mutual understanding that their needs came second to the children's needs. Both agreed it was not important to have what they wanted if it was at the expense of the children not getting what they needed. Rosa knew things like home remodeling and trips as a couple would come later after the children's expenses were paid.

The goals of these couples were to share their lives and to also have a strong sense of family. There was an understanding and acceptance that family came first and family was part of what made them a whole couple. For all of these couples, the root of having a strong couple relationship was enhanced by eating meals as a family, vacationing together, and being at events as a family.

CHAPTER 6

Understanding There Are Differences in Who They Are

Rule # 5:

Understanding and
accepting, compromising
and conceding, are positive
parts of the relationship,
and are not about losing,
but about preserving
the relationship

In this chapter you will meet;

- *Jane and Gabriel, Caucasian woman and first-generation, Mexican-American man 17 Years of Marriage*

- *Adam and Mary, Caucasian couple 25 Years of Marriage*

- *Ruben and Rosa, Hispanic couple 26 Years of Marriage*

- *David and Betty, Caucasian couple 51 Years of Marriage*

- *Daisy and Ben, Caucasian couple 25 Years of Marriage*

There are many areas of differences for couples; personality differences, their own understanding of their role as parent, how they experience extended family, and how they organize their financial responsibilities. These areas create difficulties and detract from the couple's ability to enjoy each other. However, the couples in my study were able to overcome these difficulties by using a natural ability to work together, assign roles, and respect each other's personalities and idiosyncrasies. They were able to change themselves rather than having to change the other person. There was a mutual understanding that by doing this, they worked as a team and created harmony in their lives. When these couples dealt with disagreements, they had a personal way of consulting with each other, which allowed them the ability to work through the problems. They seemed to have the ability to not only be aware of the issue but also be aware of a responsibility to resolving the issue and a responsibility to the relationship.

In my marriage, we would have both gotten an "F" in understanding, compromising, and conceding. These bedrock principles of a couple relationship were not present in my marriage, but they are vital competencies that are, in fact, the building blocks of all other areas of marriage. These three words—understanding compromising, and conceding—were all mentioned by the couples in this study, in various areas of their relationship. I don't think I ever thought about preserving my relationship. That does not mean I wanted it to end, but the idea of preservation was never in my concept of marriage. I was convinced that marriage just worked because you had found each other, a very naive and misguided belief. The couples in this study, however, expressed that preservation was a part of the marriage and regularly reinforced by different kinds of actions.

The couples in this study were able to embrace each other's differences with love and kindness. That is not to say that the differences did not make them frustrated, but their differences were accepted within the understanding of a healthy relationship. They practiced preservation tactics–making decisions together, giving each other space, not needing to win, giving respect, and admiration–that strengthened their understanding, compromising, and conceding.

Making Decisions Together

Making decisions together is important for the sense of unity in a marriage and is a great preservation tactic for the couple relationship. When a couple makes a joint decision, neither spouse will feel devalued or disrespected, and they will feel that there is an equal partnership and equal desire to make things work. Making decisions together came easy for the couples in the study. These couples functioned as a team, and teams work together for the good of everyone on the team. They made sure to stop before forging ahead with a decision and automatically knew that it needed to be discussed with their partner. The ability to think as a partnership came from the establishment that doing things together was in the best interest of the family. This ability to make decisions as a team stopped many of the misunderstandings and conflicts that often occur in marriage. When decision making is shared in a marriage there is a sense of being appreciated as a team member and a sense of safety that you are not being left out. Joint decision making says, "we are both important in this marriage and we both are invested."

Winning in a conflict does not mean a win for the relationship

A Learning Experience

Betty and David made decisions together for the most part. However, on one occasion David made a decision without Betty's consent to remodel one of their rental homes. He knew Betty was waiting to have work done on their home, but he felt very strongly about taking care of his tenants. This was not a new thing and had been a pattern in their lives together, but this time Betty felt hurt. Betty had been waiting to remodel their home for years, and she believed that David did not take her into consideration before he made this decision alone. However, Betty also realized that she had never ever made a case for herself, and this time was willing to do just that. This was the biggest crisis of their marriage and caused a major rift between them. Betty felt she had been deprioritized and that David was not listening to her. David's perspective was that he was doing what was best for their financial future by improving the rentals; he was protecting their investments. This was one of the few times in their lives that they had not talked through a decision that was so major. They separated for a few days.

Betty left and went to their lake house, but was surprised at how unhappy she was without David. When they came back together David was aware of how unhappy his decision had made both of them and said that he would try to take her feelings into account in the future. He committed to communicating better before making big decisions. David realized the importance of making decisions together and expressed this, and Betty accepted David's explanation. They learned from this experience how making decisions together was critical to their marriage.

Flexibility

When Ben and Daisy made decisions, Ben would give his opinion, Daisy would give hers, and then they usually went with Daisy's. They both concurred that Ben went with Daisy's decision 90% of the time, but this was not always easy for Ben. He felt that, on the small decisions, there was no reason to disagree and he was able to be flexible without becoming upset or expecting anything in return for it. Ben knew that if he really felt strongly about something and it was important enough, Daisy would consider his ideas. Daisy recognized that Ben was the flexible one in decision making, and knew that if Ben wanted to further discuss something, then it was important.

On important decisions, if they did not understand each other's opinions, they would wait an hour and then come back to talk about the issue. They had a system that worked for them and they were able to harmoniously navigate their differences. Ben knew that Daisy had strong opinions and that it was not about him. He conceded on issues that he did not feel strongly about. When Ben was ready to buy a new car, Daisy only had a little input. She was able to see that it was not going to be about her making the decision this time, but about Ben deciding what he wanted.

Giving Each Other Space as Part of Compromising

It was clear in the study that this was a major factor in the couple's relationship and a component of working through the difficulties. We all need time for ourselves to decompress, recharge, and find clarity and we need to accept that for our spouse this is no different. Find what "giving each other space" looks like in your relationship and make sure to actually do it! Being able to have time away from each other before the escalation of a conflict allows the spouse to question their own role in the conflict and also examine what good comes out of the conflict. They have time to reflect on how they can do their part in de-escalating the conflict and ask themselves important questions like Does holding on to my belief add to the good of the relationship? What role am I playing in this conflict? Am I understanding my partner's ideas? Am I seeing this as a personal attack? Am I blending the couple relationship and the conflict? At this point the move away from each other is about preparing for a compromise; this space allows the time to evaluate what needs to be done, plan a compromise and then execute it.

**It is okay to concede it gives you the opportunity
to put greater value on the relationship**

15 Minutes

Ruben came home from work later than Rosa, and when he got home, Rosa was ready to spend time together. However, Ruben needed time before he was able to talk about the natural issues in a marriage—finances, emotions, children. Rosa was able to accept and understand this and they came to an agreement that Ruben would have 15 minutes to clear his mind and relax when he first came in. She would make sure the kids gave Ruben the time he needed to recharge. She knew her husband well, and that 15 minutes alone made a huge difference in how Ruben would handle the stress of everyone else's day! Ruben was able after his decompression time, to make rational decisions, and to listen to the rest of the family. It also allowed him to better deal with disagreements and work towards an understanding, and if necessary a compromise.

In Tune

Marcus and Maria could read each other and knew when they needed to be alone. They did not push each other and were in tune with each other's needs, even if there was not an obvious reason for them needing space. If Maria was busy with work, Marcus would be aware and make sure not to feel that she was ignoring him. It was not uncommon for Maria to have to take a phone call when they were spending time together. Marcus was very aware of the commitment Maria had to her work and this was nothing personal. Maria's work was not seen as a problem, she could take a call at 6 am or 6 pm and it was all part of an acceptance and understanding they had of each other's roles. However, Marcus knew if he was feeling that work had to wait, he could tell her and she would make him the priority in that moment. Both of them had learned to compromise over time. They were comfortable with each and comfortable that there were times when they would irritate each other, but, realized that it was just the grind of life. They were confident that they had a strong relationship and nothing would change that.

Not Needing to Win

When a spouse needs to win, what happens? This is a very hard area for most couples to understand. When both partners in a relationship refuse to give up the belief that, "I am right," the push and pull begins. There are always 3 sides to every story. The one that each spouse tells and the one that can work for the couple. Not winning is not about losing or being less of a person, but about accepting that the relationship is of greater value than scoring a win. When a spouse wins because of submissive acceptance, the problem silently remains and creates a sense of begrudging resentment. However, when not winning is about preservation of the couple relationship, and for the good of the family, then the ability to process not winning becomes easier and de-escalates the possibility of the conflict fracturing the couple relationship. Understanding and compromise win out.

Avoiding Damage

Ben and Daisy expressed that no matter how much resolve there seemed for one partner to win, it was more important to be able to calculate how the interaction was going to affect their marriage and come to an agreement that worked for them. They wanted the relationship to continue without irreconcilable damage. For Ben, he understood it was easier to give in to her way than to fight for his way. He did not see it as losing, but as coming to an agreement, working through it, and avoiding damage. Ben was not an argumentative person by nature. He was calm at work and with friends, so it was easy for him when Daisy wanted her way, to be a listener and to understand the situation with a calmness that worked for the two of them. Ben was not a pushover; he wanted his relationship to be a priority.

Don't Sweat the Small Stuff

Carmen and Henry trusted that their disagreements could be worked out by one of them conceding. They had a respect for each other that allowed them not to need to win. Carmen let Henry be the main decision maker and felt that the relationship was stronger when they allowed one person to take control. She found it easy not to "sweat the small stuff" and accepted Henry's decisions. For Carmen this was a time in her life that she felt that she belonged to a family, her family. Hence it was about making it work. By not getting upset at every little thing she was able to enjoy her husband and family, and feel safe in her relationship.

Burden of Anger

David and Betty found that carrying around anger was just a burden. They agreed that disagreements needed to be worked out. They put so much work into the marriage and knew that letting disagreements fester would only drive them to divorce! Divorce was not an option. They knew that a relationship was not about the individual, so they did not feel they needed to always win. They both did things that made them mad at each other, but in the end, they trusted and cared about each other. In 50 years of marriage, they had had their fair share of situations where they did not like each other and had disagreements, but they had learned that the bond between them was stronger than continuing a discourse.

Giving Respect

If there was one trait that was present in all areas of these couples' lives, it was respect. Anger often makes couples less respectful and can cause arguments to become degrading attacks. During disagreements, no matter how uncomfortable or distressing, the couples were able to maintain respect. This is a strong factor in being able to create a place of wellbeing, feeling free to be yourself emotionally and physically, and in forming an accepting tolerance of each other. The ability to hold on to respect allowed the couple to never lose sight of the fact that they were partners, even during difficult times. There was an understanding that they did not shout at each other or use foul language to hurt the other person. Although, at times, the difficulties felt overwhelming, they were always able to get through the issue by reflecting on the reality, which was the strength of the commitment and the respect they had for each other.

Through all the difficulties it is so important to hold on to respect for each other no matter how hard at times

Increasing the Love

Jackson and Sheila were aware that there was a need for calm when talking through a disagreement. They never raised their voices at each other and never went to bed upset. They respected each other too much to stay mad or intentionally hurt each other. They felt that using bad language would only hurt the relationship and did nothing to heal the wound. They felt a responsibility to speak respectfully to each other because of their love for one another. They believed it was important to let each other know their love and never left the house without kissing each other or saying "I love you." Even on the days when they felt frustrated at each other, they kept this ritual. This affection, kindness, and respect increased the love they had for each other and was a major healer for both of them. It was not always like this. When they first married Jackson ran with his friends and hung out drinking, and running around at night with a bad crowd that disrespected women. He had not grown up seeing respect for women. It took time, patience and a desire to save the marriage by Sheila that helped Jackson make the right choices. She did not just focus on the negative, but had the ability to see the good in him. Jackson could not see it at first, but Shelia helping him see how his actions were hurting her and the family. Once he realized this, he was able to turn his life around.

Emotional Thread

Shaan and Azam could not remember a time when there was any yelling or hurtful things being said in their marriage. They worked hard to be open and honest and that trust was important. They had an emotional thread and a genuine sense of happiness when together. Their relationship was based on a give and take, compassion and most importantly, respect. Because of this, their love for each other just kept growing. For them, culturally there was always an importance put on respect. Even when they felt the other person was not right, there was a way of addressing this that allowed respect to remain. Both Shaan and Azam grew up in families that upheld this view. They knew how to talk to each other and did not need to wavier as they did not see the need to hurt each other. As an arranged marriage they started their life differently than couples who had dated first. They bought into their marriage the expectations of their elders; hence they started off with a set of expectations which included respect, and the importance of making a marriage work.

Admiration

All the couples in the study spoke in a positive way about each other. When addressing how they felt about their spouse, it was not uncommon for the couple to use endearing words and validate each other. There was a softness and a kindness that was present when they spoke about each other. The couples had an admiration for each other and this was part of the stability of the marriage. It was apparent that admiration had a sense of importance in the relationship working. The relationship was part of what defined the couples, and the relationship was important enough that a healthy anxiety and fear of damaging the relationship was present.

Public Affection

Jane and Gabriel tried to always show respect and admiration for each other. They were both in their second marriage and know this level of respect was needed for a successful marriage. Gabriel admired how Jane expressed her love in the things she did for his friends, being a wonderful hostess and caring for their needs. When his friends came over he felt she uplifted his friends and affirmed him as her spouse. It was not uncommon for Gabriel to turn up with friends on short notice and for Jane to make them feel welcome with food and hospitality. For Jane when she did this for her husband, there was a pride of showing him how much she cared and loved him. Even when together in public, there was always a sense of loving admiration. Coming from two marriages that did not work, they had past experiences they did not want to relive. Their goal in this marriage was to grow love, not diminish the love they had for each other.

Health Scare

Ben loved Daisy and acknowledged that he did not show it all the time because he assumed she knew. Ben and Daisy were often physically apart because both of their jobs required traveling constantly, so planning time for the two of them was a huge achievement. After much planning, they went to Hawaii together and they were both excited about the trip. However, when they arrived, Ben only wanted to sleep or spend time by the pool. Daisy felt disappointed and irritated that he was so laid back on their first vacation, but reminded herself it was a vacation for both of them.

They spent a week there quietly and within days of returning Ben had a heart attack. Daisy had no idea that Ben was quiet because he wasn't feeling well, and Ben didn't tell her because he did not want to ruin her trip. After Ben recovered they became more aware of how much love and admiration they had for each other. Just the thought of losing Ben was overwhelming for Daisy.

They realized that they needed to communicate better, and share more when things were not right. This scare reminded them how much they appreciated and needed each other. They appreciated just how much they meant to each other, and realized this health crisis had drawn them closer together.

CHAPTER 7

Differences and Remembrance

Rule # 6:

Remember the Past and How You Came Together as a Way to Accept Your Differences

In this chapter you will meet

- *Adam and Mary, Caucasian couple 25 Years of Marriage*

- *Jane and Gabriel, Caucasian woman and first generation*

- *Carmen and Henry Carmen is Hispanic and Henry is Caucasian 15 Years of Marriage*

- *Mexican American man 17 Years of Marriage*

- *Sheila and Jackson African American couple 33 Years of Marriage*

- *Ruben and Rosa, Hispanic couple 26 Years of Marriage*

- *David and Betty, Caucasian couple 51 Years of Marriage*

- *Daisy and Ben, Caucasian couple 25 Years of Marriage*

The major culprit in divorce is differences! Yes, some marriges need to end for good reasons, but many end because differences breed anger, contempt, and ultimately the thought of leaving. Differences are about who we are, what we believe, and what we have learned before we enter the relationship. These differences often feel like a personal attack during times of conflict in a marriage. We need to understand that differences are not always planned by your spouse to hurt you. They are just differences in who you are. When couples are able to remember their past and see each other's differences as just that, they are able to change the way they think rather than wait around for the other person to change.

Differences

Where do I start! If I had to pick one reason for my divorce it would be differences. Differences that were never discussed or understood. Differences that made each of us look uncaring and selfish in the other person's eyes. Differences down to the little things like laundry or the idea of what food meant! I love cooking because it was such a big part of my childhood. Italian mothers make sure you Munga, Munga, Munga (Eat, Eat, Eat). For me, it is a reflection of the way you take care of the ones you love. During my marriage,

I would take great pride in preparing food. Dinners were always important to me and it was important that Ron loved what I made him. However, on many occasions he would walk in and say he had eaten or had a late lunch and wasn't hungry. We never reached an understanding of the different meaning food had for each of us. To Ron, you ate when you were hungry. He was oblivious to the significance cooking had for me and I had no idea that he did not have the same understanding as I did. We did not take time to ask each other why we were angry and figure out how our actions affected each other. We did not try to learn each other's point of view and we remained frustrated. We were always fighting over our differences, and in the end, we got divorced.

We are all different and our differences make us unique

We are all different and often we pick a mate that compliments those differences. A wife that is outgoing might have been drawn to her husband because he was quiet and calm. An outwardly affectionate husband might be drawn to a wife that is more reserved. However, sometimes the very things we are drawn to are the very things that pull us apart. The differences become our bones of contention. The outgoing wife becomes the loud, overbearing wife, the affectionate husband becomes the insecure, demanding husband. Time can corrode a couple's ability to be accepting, but it is important to remember that your differences truly do complement each other. The couples in this study were able to be accepting of the differences they had with their partner. They were aware that they were different people and that these differences were part of the person they loved.

Introverts and Extroverts

Adam was an introvert and Mary was an extrovert. They had extremely different personalities; Mary's outgoing and sociable personality was in direct conflict with Adam's more reserved personality. Mary would volunteer them both for everything and anything, as she loved caring for others. Adam was able to understand that Mary needed to be social and had an accepting tolerance of Mary's vivacious personality. He tolerated volunteering, and when Adam felt it was too much, Mary accepted that Adam was not available. She understood Adam's need to recharge and take breaks from social outings. Mary was able to stay busy on her own when Adam was not available physically or emotionally.

During little league the school needed volunteers to work the field, Mary had Adam's name at the top of the list. Adam often went along with all the activities, but this one day he had had enough! He felt that he was not going to do it. Although the school expected the volunteers to turn up, he was not going. Mary felt uncomfortable that they were not on the same page this time, as more often than not, he just went along. This was different. He told her he was tired and that she needed to handle it this time. It did not take Mary long to make the decision to accept his answer and she went in his place. It was one of the first times that he did not do something that was so major in her view.

In their discussion after the game, Adam told her that he did not want to be signed up all the time, and Mary was able to see that her desire to be helpful didn't necessarily reflect Adams desires. This was a good growing period for both of them, and a chance to reevaluate their personality differences and to come to an understanding.

Plans or No Plans

Gabriel was a planner and Jane did things by the seat of her pants. From the beginning of their marriage, Gabriel and Jane had to learn how to work through their different personalities by developing an accepting tolerance. They had an understanding that they were very different when it came to planning even the smallest thing, and this understanding helped them work around the difference. Jane understood that Gabriel was a product of Catholic school, the military, and an engineering degree. His past had made him very methodical. Jane also recognized the impact of Gabriel's early upbringing as well as her own. Jane grew up with flexibility and Gabriel with a very structured family. She knew Gabriel preferred plans to spontaneous action, so she left Gabriel in charge of planning as a way of accepting his personality. However, if something was important to Jane, Gabriel would concede, even if there were no plans made. This did not always sit well with Gabriel, but he knew it was part of accepting each other.

With the arrangements for their upcoming October anniversary, Jane did not want it planned to death. She wanted to fly out to New England and have fun spontaneously. Gabriel, on the other hand, being the organizer he was, could not stop thinking that October was the height of the season and they would not get a room short notice. However, he deferred to Jane on this one. Gabriel agreed to not make plans, though it was hard for him to let go of the control. He was aware that most people booked hotels in this area 6 months in advance to be sure to get a room.

Unable to completely conceal his concerns he told Jane that if they did not get a room they would have to sleep in the car! And she said that was fine. Even when the plans went awry and the hotel room was iffy, he accepted the situation, but with a little bit of "told you so!" He was able to say to himself in the grand scheme of things, "Did it really matter?" Whatever they were going to experience they were going to be together, which was the whole point of the anniversary trip. He kept his cool because he was able to love his wife with all her differences, more than he loved getting his own way. He also got to say "TOLD YOU SO!"... Which she took with a smile.

Cultural Differences

In the beginning of Henry and Carmen's marriage, they had to find out how their different cultures affected who they were in the relationship. They did not always understand each other's cultures, but they both had great respect for each other's cultural norms. They were less involved in Carmen's Hispanic heritage, but the amount of involvement worked for both of them. They accepted and respected each other, and happily lived in a blend of cultures that was right for their family. Henry did not like change, and always wanted the traditional American-style of celebrating Thanksgiving and Christmas. When they were with Carmen's family, he tolerated the different foods and cultural experience, but Carmen was aware he missed the traditional holidays. Being aware of his need for a traditional holiday she had no problem spending most of these holidays with his family and knew it was not because he did not like her family. Henry was aware of this and it only made him appreciate her more.

There was an appreciation that was evident with all the couples, that their own quirkiness or rigid needs were accepted in their marriage. It was obvious that the acceptance of who they were by their spouse created a profound sense of love and a deep sense of security in the marriage, and started the journey into intimacy. Although the couples reported being frustrated by certain behaviors and habits that belonged to their spouse, they were able to work through it without damaging the relationship.

Remembering the past

For all the couples there was an anchor back to the past that, although not always consciously, came out in many subtle ways. Moments of remembering happy events helped them get through tougher situations. The individual's idea that "my marriage works," was supported by the individual being able to reflect on the good times and the reasons they were with their spouse. It was possible for these couples to use the good they remembered about their spouse to dissipate the anger or frustration of a negative situation. They could find the good in the other person and keep the issue from getting out of hand.

Remember the times that made you laugh and smile
these are what bought you together

Looking Back

Betty and David often looked back on their life together and agreed that they had complemented each other. They felt they had the same vision when they started dealing with all aspects of finance and children. Betty saw David as a hard worker and they created their life together. They remembered being so young when they got married and trying to survive. They remembered caring for each other and how the good life grew. Their reflection on their past made them realize that they would not leave each other, no matter what. David felt that in the beginning it was all about sex and this held them together, which was then cemented by having children. Betty believed that they did not always understand each other every day and that they were always two separate people trying to do something together.

She believed they had no idea what to do when they got married. They remembered not feeling unified at the beginning of their marriage. She was pregnant at 19 which did not give them enough time to get to know each other before parenting. She felt they were uneducated about life. Betty remembered that they did not ask anyone to help as they felt they shouldn't ask questions. However, they started off with tolerance, compromise, and patience, and while marriage was a shock for both of them, 51 years later they are still making it work. They reflected on what they did not know in the beginning of their marriage and both agreed they had grown The happiest time for both of them was when they were busy building their company and found that they had similar traits and work ethics. They always knew it would just get better. Looking back David savors the memory of that cute girl he knew he wanted to kiss.

Businesses

Marcus and Maria would get discouraged about their marriage at times, but they remembered the 32 years they shared together and the love they still had after all those years. Maria remembered the man that she had fallen in love with, and all the worry and adversity they had faced together. Marcus remembered when they first met, he knew that this woman was the one he wanted. Even though their situations were so different -she a white collar worker, and him a blue! -- They did not let that stop them. In Marcus's eyes Maria today was just as beautiful as she was in the beginning of their marriage. They both remembered the hard times in building two businesses together and had many memories of the terrible situations they had to get through. They believed if they could survive that, they could survive anything! All the memories were part of what made the marriage work and held the family together.

Staying in Love

Jane believed that she made the decision to stay in love, and to pay attention to the things she appreciated in the first place. She had one failed marriage and had learned many lessons of what not to do. Jane stayed committed to this second marriage and after 17 years, still had a crush on Gabriel. It was not hard for Jane to say nice things about Gabriel to her friends; actually, she enjoyed sharing the nice things they did for each other. She took pride in having a relationship that worked and created an environment that allowed them both to stay in love.

Jane reflected on the man she married and saw that same man was in her life today. Gabriel was a man she could trust, a hard worker, a good provider, responsible with money and had a big heart. For Gabriel, he never doubted Jane's love for him. When he was asked about what kept them together through the bad times, he would say it was because he was committed to his wife. They reminded themselves of their love by always talking positively and lovingly about each other and even when it was difficult and they were tested. They both had made mistakes in their previous marriages and had no intention of letting this one go.

Faith

Faith is a very personal journey and many of the couples in this study grew up with faith or found faith as adults. No matter how faith came into their lives, it was part of how they dealt with their day-to-day experiences with family, spouse, and life. Faith was a part of the way they processed their misunderstandings and allowed them to have acceptance through tolerance for their partner. If you are a person of faith, then understanding how faith integrates into your marriage is important. For some of these couples, it was possible to not only develop an acceptance through tolerance of the other person, but to add another dynamic of intimacy in their understanding of what faith meant to the marriage and to themselves.

Prayer and Decisions

Faith played a role in Adam and Mary's decision making. They prayed together for the answer to tough decisions, and this was an important part of their relationship. Faith was a way to understand each other with help from the Lord, and they felt prayer helped them be accepting of their differences. However, it had been a journey. They were both raised Catholic, but Adam did not attend church in school or college. Mary was a devout Catholic and spent time in bible study as well as going to mass weekly. After moving to California from the Midwest, they both attended a non-denominational church. Mary was very uncomfortable not attending Catholic Church, but realized her husband was seeking something and she wanted to join him on that journey. She went with him and after a time realized that it worked for both of them and she found peace in her new denomination.

Difference in Faith

Carmen was the only faith-based person in her family. While Henry did not believe, he understood this was where they had differences and that it was important for him to have an accepting tolerance and allow his wife to express her faith. This allowed them to navigate their differences in faith without tension. This understanding and acceptance did not just happen, Carmen had spent many years early in the marriage defending her faith. Henry believed that organized religion was trouble and did not want his children growing up in a faith-based home. Because of his desire to have a happy home and an understanding of his wife's needs he stopped putting up a fight. He learned to self-reflect on what it meant for the family, and over the 15 years together faith became less of a problem for him. He had come to the understanding that faith made his wife happy. During a fight with cancer, Carmen turned to faith more than ever. Henry was aware that she got strength from her faith and decided to join her in her faith. This connection added to both of their ability to get through the illness, and strengthened the bond in their marriage.

Faith plays a powerful role for many couples had has the ability to protect the couple relationship

Faith and Appreciation

Shelia turned to the word of God and believed in God's direction. Faith taught her to love and respect her partner. Shelia believed when you had respect for each other and God, a couple could grow together through any difficulties. She felt that, through faith, life's blessings were not taken for granted. Jackson came from a family with no faith affiliations. For Jackson, there were very few times he went to church, and learning about faith was not a part of his childhood, nor his adult life. Sheila knew that Jackson did not have the same faith that she did, but let Jackson approach faith in his own way. They appreciated each other's differences in faith and Sheila used her faith to increase her love for Jackson. In time Jackson came to see what faith did for his wife and how it gave her the strength to work through anything. He was able to start going to church with her and slowly began to understand what faith meant to his family as a whole. It was a journey they took together and continue on that same journey still.

CHAPTER 8

Acceptance through Tolerance as an Organic Process in the Marriage

Not About Changing The Other Person, But Changing You

The phrase, "acceptance through tolerance," has popped up repeatedly throughout this book, but what does that really mean? "Acceptance through tolerance is being able to tolerate what you regard as an unpleasant behavior of your partner, and understanding the deeper meaning of that behavior; it is a letting go of trying to change each other"(Christensen, 2013). Acceptance through tolerance is a profound type of acceptance that allows couples to experience marital satisfaction in their relationship and build intimacy.[10]

Acceptance is not about changing your partner to fit what you want; this is a false idea of acceptance that many couples have. Acceptance through tolerance is about adjusting your mindset so that you understand and appreciate who your spouse is. While not always apparent, acceptance through tolerance creates change in the relationship which, in turn, increases marital satisfaction. When couples give up trying to change each other, and experience their partner's difficult behavior without trying to escape from it, they integrate an understanding into the relationship which decreases the toxicity of a conflict. Acceptance through tolerance is not achieved by submissive acceptance—that is, allowing toxic behavior unquestioningly—but by couples being able to understand the differences in who they are, and how they experience a situation. This acceptance provides the couple the ability to see each other's behavior in a larger context, and to appreciate the value and importance this behavior has for the relationship.

[10] Christensen, A., Doss, B. D., & Jacobson, N. S. (2013). Reconcilable differences: Rebuild your relationship by rediscovering the partner you love - Without losing yourself.

It is often the misunderstanding of an event or of each other that creates the emotionally driven behavior that fuels the breakdown in the couple relationship. Acceptance through tolerance is not about banishing conflict, but about helping couples tame the conflict so they can see the conflict in a more dispassionate way. By doing this, they are able to repair the relationship.[11]

There are many ways in which this phenomenon manifested itself in these interviews: respect, commitment, verbal expressions of love, selflessness, appreciation, conceding, understanding, kindness, and admiration. These characteristics do not stand alone; they are interwoven into the fabric of the experiences the couples have together. Respect was at the foundation of the experiences and remained constant no matter how hard decision making was, or how numerous the differences were. This respect was not only for the person but for the very foundation of the relationship. The powerful investment in each other and the relationship was greater than any conflict.

However, respect could not sustain itself without the other characteristics by its side. Commitment and understanding forged a unity that allowed an accepting tolerance, even in the throngs of discord. Conceding in an argument, and not having to win, helped de-escalate these times of conflict. Conceding is a kind of selflessness that is a part of the phenomenon of acceptance through tolerance when the unity of the relationship is being tested. This selflessness was the ability to look within, question the role they played, and to find what was needed to sustain the common good of the couple relationship—asking, "Do I need to win this argument?" At the same time, compromise, rather than surrender, was a building block in the relationships. These ways of accepting through tolerance maintain the integrity of a

---

[11] Christensen, A., Doss, B. D., & Jacobson, N. S. (2013). Reconcilable differences: Rebuild your relationship by rediscovering the partner you love - Without losing yourself.

relationship; they are victories for a couple that comes from understanding and love, interwoven with respect.

The couples in my study found that acceptance through tolerance created change in the relationship, which increased their marital happiness. They were able to review how they felt and see how they affected the relationship. They understood the difference between personal attack and difference of opinion. Their ability to review each other in a more compassionate way came from a sensitivity they had to each other and highlighted the importance of the preservation of the couple relationship. The couples were aware of their own role when it came to making demands on their spouse. They were able to correct and repair before escalation took place by being interactive and perceptive in the couple relationship. Acceptance was the reason these couples could repair the relationship in times of conflict. This acceptance of each other and the ability to understand the issues, without damaging the relationship, did not come by a submissive acceptance, but by the couples being able to understand their differences in who they were and how they experienced a situation. They were able to see each other's behavior in a larger context and to appreciate the value and importance this behavior had on the relationship. The couples were willing to accept themselves and the other person for who they were. There was an understanding that they were different in certain areas, but alike in other ways.

When it came to disagreements these couples were aware that being spiteful and combative did nothing to allow them to resolve the issues. They realized that staying focused on what was happening in the disagreement allowed them to resolve the issue without damaging the couple relationship. The couples were able to acknowledge the negative situation in the relationship and work to reframe these situations for a more understanding outcome. They looked for ways to resolve, rather than focusing on "winning." The ability to have an accepting tolerance of the disagreements came from a strong sense of responsibility to staying in the marriage, and for some couples the obligation they had to their faith. For all the couples there was a motivation and desire to preserve the marriage and the family.

We need to appreciate that we may not always agree with our spouse. We will have arguments, frustration, and discord, but if we remember our desire not to damage the relationship, there will remain a power to repair. The rules of engagement are clear and will keep a marriage healthy; six rules to maintain and six important areas in our couple relationships. But, without acceptance through tolerance, in following all the rules, in our day-to-day preservation, and in all of our actions, we will not have the power to repair.

The Good Marriage, Making It Work!

As we all know if we are married or have been married, it is not easy. We enter this union with the expectations of making a lifelong commitment to the other person. Then life happens. The curve balls come around the corner, work takes its toll, finances create stress and worry, and all the while we have to keep our eye on the relationship and the commitment we made to another person. Often our own sense of misunderstanding of the situations creates a theme of discontent that begins to grow in the relationship and starts the void that begins the downhill slide of the relationship. But, it does not have to be this way. We just have to learn to accept that there are many moving parts to a couple relationship. We have to learn not only to understand the present but to acknowledge and learn from the past. No matter how hard and difficult a situation, respect must remain at the forefront of acceptance through tolerance.

Do not be afraid of making it work, keeping it intact, and believing in preservation. A marriage can still be a great marriage, even when a couple is just trying to maintain. A great marriage does not mean there are no wounds or trying times for the relationship, but rather that partners work on healing and remain stronger than the dissension. Being able to remain intact comes from understanding that the relationship is made up of many things: appreciation, respect, history, intimacy, the family, and a selflessness from both sides to remain together.

We are together in these conflicts and these issues are ours as couples. We are united in love, respect, responsibility, and commitment to our lives together and to make it work through sickness and in health. The commitment we made to each other when we chose each other is one that can only grow and become stronger, with understanding that we are in this for good, and remembering what makes the relationship work—the Rules of Engagement!

CHAPTER 9

The Tools of Engagement

What Can You Do to Change Your Relationship?

Yes, these couples in the study made it work, and yes they have great advice. However, in the thick of a difficult marriage or a marriage that is of course, how do you find your way back to the happiness that you once had with your spouse? How are you able to do the work that would allow a long-term, happy marriage? In the tools of engagement you will find ways to help you to get back onto the right track and build that relationship that will last a lifetime.

I believe in every relationship there is a grain of sand, just like if you were sitting on the beach enjoying a delicious sandwich, and you came across a little bit of sand in the sandwich; you would probably keep eating. If you were walking down the street and you realized there was a pebble in your shoe you would have to stop for a moment or two to take it out, but would then keep on walking. If you came across a large rock on your path, you might have someone help you move it, it might take a little longer, but you would still continue on. However, when you come up against a boulder there is no way to move it and you have to turn around and give up. This is what marriage is like. We can all deal with the little things and invest in getting through them. When things bother us we can talk to friends or family and find a way to keep going forward. But when they become too big it often seems like there is no way out except to leave. The conflicts have become too great and the losses too many.

Conflict
Conflict, as we described in earlier chapters, comes dressed in many different robes! To be able to understand your own conflict you need to be able to identify what it looks like.

Many areas of conflict are about the areas we talked about in the rules of engagement: extended family, finances, parenting, time together, and differences.

Areas that are also affected by conflict are tasks at home, how we perceive affection, temperament, goals, trust, employment, the use of alcohol or drugs in a relationship, and the level of our own intimacy. In life there are many challenges and we work through them. If not physically or emotionally dangerous, none of our challenges should be more important to us than preserving our marriage. Often we do not see our part in the conflict as we so often can only see the other person's deficits. Looking at what your role in conflict is and what you believe your partner's role is, is the first step to change.

Look at what your role is in the conflict. Do you blame, and find fault with your partner's actions? Do you nag as you think this will guilt your partner into submission? Do you try and persuade to show you are right? Do you demand that they see your side and only your side? Do you push your partner until you both escalate and argue? And finally, where does this get you? And what does it do for you? It does not create harmony, it does not add to the advancement of understanding and loving each other, but rather it often goes into the bank of discontent. It sits there waiting for the next conflict where you will be more prepared to use anything to win.

I was a very rich spouse as my bank was full! I put everything in so that I could bring it out and use it for ammunition in the next conflict. And where did it get me! It made it easier to dislike my spouse and made it harder to find any good in him. I was always looking to change him or help him see how he could change, such as paying me more attention than his job and friends, holding my hand or a simple thing such as wearing his wedding ring. I believed that not wearing the ring meant he was not committed to the relationship and with all the other stuff in my bank I had to be right. What I never looked at was his side. I never looked at the other things that he was doing to show me he was invested. I did not know how he felt about the ring and he did not know it had a symbolic value to me that it did not have for him.

When you can see your role in the conflict then you have the opportunity to change yourself. Rather than waiting for your spouse to change you can contemplate what is going on in the issue at hand, rather than withdraw from the bank of discontent to help support your side of the conflict. Instead, you could open a saving bank and drop in there all the things that you love and care about your spouse and help that account to keep growing

What Player Are You in the Conflict?

The Pursuer

Everyone has a style of interaction in a relationship. More often than not the style of each spouse is always the same in the conflict, just with a different conflict script. Are you the spouse that pursues? How does this change anything? Do you find fault in your spouse, do you criticize and demand that they do what you want, and does this escalate into a conflict that is out of control? When you behave the same way each time do you get a different response? Or just a repeat of the same old, same old? This in and of itself is a good reason to look at your role in the conflict, and to consider how, and why you take on that role.

What emotion is driving you? How do you feel at that moment? Nagging is not just a behavior, it is part of the personality that believes if I go long enough I will get appeased, my will, will be done, and I can feel that I have achieved what needs to be done. I will win this one. But there is a price to pay, as nagging, criticizing, and demanding become expected and the spouse that is on the receiving end cannot look at the real issue, but only figure out the fastest way to get out of the situation. Before you nag, criticize or demand, think "What am I feeling right now and what is the emotion behind the feeling? Am I feeling unappreciated, invalidated or once again unimportant?" How can you see this differently? Are you feeling this is a personal attack, or is it really about an issue that is being discussed? How can you be frustrated about the issue, rather than personally hurt by the issue? If you can remove the issue from the personal and deal with the issue the cost to the relationship will be decreased.

Pursuer: criticizing, showing that you are right
pointing out the others faults

The Withdrawer

Or are you someone that withdraws and avoids the conflict, dismisses or diminishes the other person? This is a common role in couple's relationship. Typically one of the partners would have this role while the other a pursuer. It is not uncommon for a withdrawer to try and avoid the fallout during a conflict or try to dismiss, or make less of the seriousness of the situation. The withdrawer will find a way to escape the conflict, either by shutting down any communication, or by leaving. It is very hard to be with a withdrawer if you are not one, as you will feel that nothing gets resolved.

For the spouse that is not a withdrawer there is a sense of never being able to work through the conflict, and the frustration mounts. Whether withdrawer or pursuer, if you can identify your role, you can be more aware of your part in conflict, and can begin to make changes in how you handle the conflict cycle.

The Withdrawer: avoiding, denying, evading, shutting down

Triangulating

We all know what a triangle looks like; it has three sides. Hence in a couple relationship where one spouse or the other brings a third person into the mix of a conflict, they have triangulated. Spouses will use the children, extended family and friends to make their point stronger. It can be very lonely to have to deal with issues with your spouse, and it often seems like a good idea to air these grievances or issues and get support. However there is a difference in venting for your own good, and bringing a person into side with you. When we have someone on our side then we have double the investment in winning or convincing the other person they are wrong. Although it might support your side it does nothing for the relationship. Conflict is tough, and when we don't know where to go we really believe we need to keep airing the issue with others. Unfortunately, this will often only increase the turmoil, and can result in others in being biased against your spouse. What happens when you have been able to resolve the issue, and the information that you shared is still out there? I believe for many couples, it feels like the natural way to go; why would we not want to be understood, since our spouse doesn't understand us? And if everyone agrees with you then you must be right. Who else would see your side if not for your family and friends?

However, in every situation there are three sides to every conflict. And if you keep the issue between the two of you, without including others, then you have more hope of viewing the issue in a constructive way and working to a resolution. You will have a greater hope of seeing the third side of the conflict, the part where you can understand each other's emotions and views. Sticking to how you feel personally about the issue, keeping the focus on the issue at hand and keeping it between the two of you will not only help you find understanding, but will also help you learn to work through the conflict that is taking place in that moment. It will stop you from wanting to go to your bank of discontent and make a withdrawal. And by keeping the issue the issue you will be able to resolve that issue, one way or another.

Triangulating : telling others about the conflict to gain support for your side, getting help to change the outcome for your benefit

What Kind Of Disposition Do You Have In The Relationship?

Many times when we meet someone there is something about their disposition that attracts us. We often see these characteristics as the ones we want in a relationship and we go for it; then comes marriage. When conflict and issues appear in our relationship we often see the sympathetic, kind spouse in a less favorable light. The once solid sympathetic spouse can now seem weak or out of touch. Or that outgoing, disorganized, quirky spouse is now seen as lazy and lacking in self-discipline. It is amazing how allowing conflict to take its toll on the marriage allows the spouse that we once loved to metamorphosed into someone that we cannot understand, and many times during conflict, even dislike. The very things we loved now are parts of what we end up not liking. How does this happen?

Ron loved my outgoing personality and that was part of what drew him to me, but at the end labeled me outspoken and conflictual. What I saw in him was a quiet, solid, understanding and tolerant man that I could trust. At the end I saw him as unresponsive, uncommunicative, and intolerant of who I was. How do these changes take place? No one waves a wand and we change. These changes build up as we invest in the bank of discontent. It takes time for the bank to get full, but if we understood our own role rather than looking for our partner's role, we would be able to invest in the savings bank, rather than the bank of discontent.

The Fuel On The Fire

Stress

Who doesn't have stress? It is not whether we have stress, but rather what we do with it when it comes to our relationship. It is amazing when we first date the person we marry how we were able to keep the stress out of the relationship. As we get to know each other more and then marry, stress becomes a member of the family. Stress is such a consumer of our health and our wellbeing. And we are not always the guilty party when it comes to stress. Life has become a fast track to getting things done. There is the worry of debt. There are pressures from our jobs. Add to that the expectations from our children, and trying to have a relationship with the one we married. It is not surprising stress has a place at the table. When we don't talk about how we experience and handle stress, then our partner has to keep guessing.

Our spouses are not mind readers, and often the stress issue comes in sheep's clothing and upsets the couple relationship. Rather than a couple being able to know the signals, or having a system that works when stress is present, a blow-up occurs and takes its toll on the couple relationship. Both parties get hurt and angry. When couples talk about what their needs are when they are under stress, they can then support each other in that moment, rather than being offended by an outburst or trying to guess whether they have done something wrong. Talking about what your needs are before you are in the moment will only add to your spouse's ability to have a better understanding of your needs, and an accepting tolerance of what to do when stress is present.

The Emotions From Our History

We have many experiences that mold us from our family of origin before we ever married. We grew up believing a certain way, and we experienced the joys and hurts of childhood. More often than not the way we are treated by our parents when we were young is how our parents were treated in their own childhood. We know that many behaviors are passed down from generation to generation. Not all are bad behaviors; the good is also passed down with the bad. The negative experiences of our childhood often do not present themselves until they are triggered by a similar action in adulthood. A father that was very rarely home could leave a little girl feeling unlovable and abandoned by his absence. Hence when this little girl marries and her husband works late on weekends, the same feelings can be triggered, but often get labeled as something else. A husband that grew up with demanding parents whom he could never please, could have grown up always feeling like a failure and inadequate. Hence he could easily view his wife's frustration at him not getting a job finished as a judgment that he was inadequate.

These kind of situations often drive a conflict of misunderstanding; the underlying emotion is not present, just the exterior hurt. This is the time to stop and think about what is driving my anger rather than going back to the bank of discontent. Could it be that he works all those hours as he wants you to have the best, and is not abandoning you but instead is worried about the family finances? Could the frustration over the job not being finished be because she had a plan for the finished project and wanted to do her thing, rather than you being inadequate?

I remember a time that Ron built a railing off our master bedroom balcony. I was gone and when I came home he had demolished the old one and built a new one. Rather than be grateful that this job was done and appreciate that he had spent his whole day working on it, I was angry. He had not asked me what kind of balcony I wanted; he had excluded me. It was another example of how unimportant in his life I was. I went to my discontent bank account and drew out a large sum. If I could have seen this had nothing to do with me, and understood that the balcony was dangerous and that he had simply matched what was there before, I would not have felt excluded.

Growing up I often felt unimportant and excluded by my mother. I believed, (I know today this is not true), she loved my brother more. He came first. I know she loved me deeply in her own way, however, he was always made to feel more important than me. I remember a time that we were all getting ready for my nephew's wedding and I wanted to take a bath, Mom said that I wasn't allowed as we had to leave the hot water for my brother's bath. As silly as this sounds it hurt me and made me feel unimportant again. We build into our current misunderstandings the emotions that we store up from the past and our own histories. If we understand the emotion that is driving us at these times we would have an easier and less emotional time with conflict.

Lower Your Guard and Be Aware Of Your Armor

I wonder how many couples are aware of their own guard, or even believe they have one. In a conflict are you aware of that instant reaction that is present when you are triggered by your spouse? We often believe that this behavior is just a response, but is really a way of protecting ourselves. Often we are not aware that it is there, but if we stop and think about what we are feeling, and how we are responding, we might come up with a different answer. Am I in a defensive mode? Can I be open to hearing what the other person is saying or am I too busy preparing my response? What would it be like to be self-aware and then listen to the other person? What would be different? Could I focus on the issue and leave my protective armor outside?

What Can You Tolerate?

There are things that will never change in a relationship that will have to be accepted. Little traits that are part of that person, although irritating or frustrating, have nothing to do with change. Your spouse may like to go to bed early and you like to go late, or your spouse leaves a dish in the sink, which you would not do. These are the kind of situations that a couple learns to live with. The toothpaste top does not go on, or the toilet seat stays up… So many of these you can put down to being short-lived irritations, rather than life-changing issues. We are all different and we learn many things from our families of origin. I like my tea a certain way. I want fresh water in the electric kettle and before it goes on the tea bag I want it to reach a roaring boil. AND it must be poured within seconds over the bag or it has to go back on the boil. I know I cannot enjoy a cup of tea that is not made this way. It is the same in the relationship; you know the things that you have to accept even if you would like it different. In the couple relationship both need to know the difference between the real issues, and the traits that are part of their spouse.

Learning How To Talk To Each Other, and When

Talking to each other is such an important part of the couple relationship. The way in which we talk to each other is the root of many of the triggers, and when it is a difficult topic it can be the reason we put up our guard. If the same negative reaction happens every time you try and discuss a difficult or sensitive topic, then more than likely you are putting up your guard. Understanding how to talk to each other, and when is a good time, is part of the process of learning to communicate in a more understanding and accepting way.

It is essential to agree on what this looks like for both of you, and discuss what each of you needs before the situation occurs. Choose a time-out that works for both of you to de-escalate, and figure out how you will reconnect after the time-out. Think about how you can express how you feel rather than trying to express what you believe your partner has done to you. Ask yourself what you are feeling and whether it actually has to do with the issue that is presented. Is it an old wound that is opening up that is perhaps not even related? Or is this a recurring issue that has never been resolved? And is there another way that you can discuss it that would be more effective? Can you have a soft start up and talk about yourself rather than going straight to a harsh attack? Imagine what that would be like, to be able to resolve an issue rather than sweep it under the rug until the next time, or leave feeling attacked and misunderstood. You CAN change the outcome if you are able to see your role and evaluate what you are experiencing as you communicate with each other.

When Do We Need Couples Therapy?

I believe most couples seek couples therapy when they believe there is no hope and this is the last stand before the end. Finding the right couples therapist is essential to having a successful reconciliation. If you want to save the marriage but you aren't making progress going it alone, Couples therapy may be of benefit. But it is important that the therapist use an evidence –based treatment model that goes deep enough into the underlying differences and relational issues. However, there is nothing good about divorce unless you are in an abusive relationship and then it is an option. At the end of my marriage our couple's therapy was appalling! Completely rule-governed. I was told to be nicer to my husband, and he was told to show me the financial accounts, all of his accounts! I tried to be nicer and he did show me the books. He woke me up at 3 am to show me the statements (I believe in hindsight he was hoping at that time in the morning I would not recall anything the next day). It only worked for a few months, and then divorce was imminent. If we could have instead examined the way we saw each other, we would have been able to find what was driving our fear and emotions.

Couples that enter therapy with someone that uses Integrated Behavioral Couples Therapy (IBCT) http://ibct. psych.ucla.edu/therapists.html will have the opportunity to work on change-- changing how they see the relationship and their partner, not waiting for their partner to change. The couple will be able to work towards acceptance through tolerance in the relationship. There is always hope in a relationship that has gone off the rails because of communication or misunderstandings. If a couple can see through the fog of rejection and hurt and work on understanding each other, there is the opportunity to reconnect and build a happier and healthier relationship.

Forgiveness And Remembering Who You Fell In Love With and Why

Many years ago I was talking to a good friend who was a priest. He said something that I have never forgotten. He said, the greatest therapy in life is laughter! Therapy is part of the journey for a relationship that needs help from a professional. However, simply reflecting on who you married and why can be a profound journey of its own. None of us marry just for the sake of marriage; we marry the person that has triggered in us the idea that life would be better shared with this person. And there is a happiness that existed.

Do you remember when you used to laugh with your spouse, when your spouse's face made you smile, and the amazing feeling that you got when your spouse walked into a room? That feeling is still there, covered up by many layers of life. Remember that those moments can be unearthed, that the joy and happiness of the relationship that you once knew is still there. Remember the person that you fell in love with, and know that going back and seeing that person in this light will help you move closer towards forgiveness and acceptance.

You have a tool shed full of great tools so go get them and start working on your relationship!

Clorinda and James Henry O'Neill on their
honeymoon at the Trevi Fountain, Rome, 1945